Pennsylvania Apples

0 11557 02883 6

With 40 Recipes and a Guide to Festivals and Farm Markets

Kyle Nagurny

STACKPOLE
BOOKS

Published by
STACKPOLE BOOKS
5067 Ritter Road
Mechanicsburg, PA 17055
www.stackpolebooks.com

Printed in China

10 9 8 7 6 5 4 3 2 1

FIRST EDITION

Cover design by Caroline Stover

Photo Credits
Cover and pages xii, 38 (bottom right), 34–41, and 72 courtesy the U.S. Apple Association; pages ii, v, vi, 3, 5–10, 12, 15, 21, 22, 32, 34, 36, 38 (top and bottom left), 43, 44, 55, and 69 courtesy the Pennsylvania Apple Marketing Board; pages 17, 18, 24, 25, and 42 courtesy Shatzer Fruit Market; page 27 courtesy Wilma Mickey; page 29 courtesy Nona Brown; page 30 courtesy Linvilla Orchards; page 46 courtesy Knouse Foods; pages 49, 56, and 57 photos by Craig A. Benner; page 53 courtesy the Roughwood Collection; pages 64, 67, and 79 photos by Joe Cicak, the Ad Factory.

Library of Congress Cataloging-in-Publication Data

Nagurny, Kyle.
Pennsylvania apples : history and culture : with 40 recipes and a guide to festivals and farm markets / Kyle Nagurny.–1st ed.
p. cm.
ISBN 0-8117-2883-8
1. Apples–Pennsylvania. 2. Apples–Varieties–Pennsylvania. 3. Cookery (Apples) I. Title.

SB363.2.U6 N35 2002
634'.11'09748–dc21

2002021745

To the growers, pickers, packers, shippers, processors, and marketers of Pennsylvania's apple industry.

Contents

Preface

The Keystone State ranks a respectable fifth among apple-producing states in the United States. Washington, the megaleader among apple states, is most synonymous with apples, thanks to vast promotional dollars that help keep the apple-producing giant uppermost in the minds of retailers and consumers.

During the last few years, however, Pennsylvania has come into its own with a loyal following who refuse to eat apples from any other state or country. Through modest but effective efforts, Pennsylvania's apple industry is driving home the message that one of the earth's oldest fruits can compete with the best from Washington, Michigan, New York, California, or wherever the source. There's something about apples cultivated in the Keystone State that makes them hold a special place for consumers with discerning palates.

Pennsylvania apples are more than a variety of sweet and tart flavors laced inside succulent textures. They represent two, three, or more generations of tough, level-headed, and very determined farmers who love to plant things and work hard to make them grow.

History and experience have shown that apples grow best along mountain ridges protected from icy, cold winds. Pennsylvania's rolling Appalachian Mountains provide a warm, protective blanket for apple trees–at least when the weather in the mountainous regions chooses to cooperate. Sometimes a return of wintery weather in the spring can damage or destroy the beautiful, soft blossoms that promised a generous harvest. Most years, however, Pennsylvania's spring and summer envelop the trees in warm days and cool nights with ample rain to produce a perfect crop–acres upon rolling acres of red, green, and yellow fruit so abundant that the tree branches droop from the heavy burden they must bear until the apples are harvested.

This book chronicles Pennsylvania's apple history, a bountiful story that almost everyone can appreciate. It also looks at the specific apple varieties that are grown in the state, goes into the orchards to record the stories of apple growers, explores the industry as it thrives today, and ends in the kitchen with tips on storage and recipes for delicious apple entrees and desserts. For those who want to explore the apple culture firsthand, the book includes comprehensive lists of the state's apple festivals and farm markets.

Grab an apple and enjoy!

Acknowledgments

I would like to acknowledge the help and support of the following people and organizations in researching and writing this book: the Pennsylvania Apple Marketing Board; the U.S. Apple Association; the Pennsylvania Department of Agriculture; the State Horticultural Association of Pennsylvania; the Adams County Fruit Growers Association; the Adams County Historical Society; the Franklin County Horticultural Society; Shatzer's Fruit Market; Linvilla Orchards; Rice Fruit Company; Strite's Orchards; Brown's Orchard; the National Apple Museum; Joe Cicak and the Ad Factory; Don Yoder; Kyle Weaver; Amy Cooper; and my husband, Mike, daughter, Kelly, and son, Michael.

Pennsylvania's

Apple Varieties

Apple trees are closely related to such well-known fruit trees as those bearing pears, cherries, peaches, plums. All are members of the rose family, and apple blossoms are, in fact, reminiscent of wild rose blossoms. The fruits of the apple and the rose are quite similar, but apples are obviously much larger than their dry, seedy rose fruit counterparts.

There are eight thousand known varieties of apples worldwide, about twenty-five hundred of which are grown in the United States. According to the U.S. Apple Association, some one hundred varieties are grown commercially across this country, about fifteen of those account for more than 90 percent of production.

Before the 1700s, there were few apple connoisseurs. As apples became a popular dessert, however, people of "class" grew to appreciate subtle and not so subtle flavor and texture differences among varieties. British countrymen were especially keen on discerning apple varieties, based on appearance and taste, just as wine connoisseurs pride themselves in their ability to discriminate among fine wines. The English had also discovered apple desserts and learned which varieties worked best in tarts, jellies, "dainties" or tartlets, and puddings.

The varieties of good eating apples steadily increased through the eighteenth century. The English were especially fond of the Golden Pippin, a small, rich yellow, multipurpose apple with an intensely tart flavor. Golden Pippins gained popularity in other countries as well, among them, Russia, where royalty happily paid a guinea a bushel.

The French, who had favored the pear for many decades, also began to appreciate the apple for its interesting flavors and varied textures.

As the century unfolded, new apple varieties grew in popularity, including the Ribston Pippin and Margil. Both were sweeter than the Golden Pippin and offered a more complex flavor profile enjoyed by sophisticated palates.

America's only native apple variety was the Sour Crab apple. During the seventeenth and eighteenth centuries, other apple varieties were shipped to America from Europe. Apples kept well on ships sailing to the colonies and were considered a staple commodity, providing a satisfying snack to both adults and children during their difficult journey.

During the 1720s, John Bartram established the first botanical gardens in America along the Schuylkill River, where he facilitated the cultivation of different varieties. In 1759, Benjamin Franklin received a box of Newtown Pippins from an English diplomat. He and his peers liked the Pippins so well that they began growing them from seed and, later, by grafting branches onto other trees. As a proponent of the scientific aspects of grafting, Franklin inspired the Philadelphia Society for Promoting Agriculture (founded 1785), which led to the formation of the Pennsylvania Horticultural Society in 1827, believed to be the first horticultural society in the country.

As rumblings increased about a war to obtain independence from Britain and the idea gained favor among the colonists, the number of apple varieties in the New World was also increasing. By the late eighteenth century, farmers were making concerted efforts to expand the variety of apples available in the colonies, including Pennsylvania. Apple growing became more of a science, as pomologists experimented to learn what varieties worked best along which ridges of the countryside. Long before the invention of the camera, line drawings and paintings served to record differences in the appearance of various apples. Today many coffee table books offer extravagant art of various apple varieties that hold a classic and timeless beauty.

Horticulturists began to collect varieties and study their often subtle differences. Researchers enjoyed grafting new versions and cultivating higher-quality grades of apples than their ancestors had known. The Golden Noble, Irish Peach, Keswick Codlin, and Pitmaston Nonpareil were all results of careful observation and experimentation. Books about apple varieties were prevalent throughout the period.

William Coxe, a member of the Philadelphia Society for Promoting Agriculture, was most likely the first American scientist to accu-

Pennsylvania Golden Delicious apples "blush" just before harvest.

rately document apple varieties, in his 1817 book, *A View of the Cultivation of Fruit Trees and the Management of Orchards and Cider.* No doubt the initial success of Pennsylvania's commercial apple industry is at least in part attributable to Coxe, who painstakenly recorded the performance of dozens of varieties in his own experimental orchard and sold about eighty of those varieties as a part of his commercial operation.

Commercial orchards were a popular source of income for Pennsylvanians by the nineteenth century. In the 1889 proceedings of the State Horticultural Association of Pennsylvania, the Variety Committee reported that fifty-four varieties of apples were being commercially grown in the state. A record had been made from each county as to what apple varieties were currently grown. Franklin County, for example, listed Fallwater as its top market variety, followed by the York. Some of the other varieties mentioned in the report were the Red Astrachan, Summer Rambo, Winter Rambo, Maiden Blush, Baldwin, York Imperial, Grimes Golden, Winter Sweet Paradise, and Ewalt.

Although Europeans had their own sophisticated array of apple varieties, they also enjoyed imports of Yankee apples. Between 1875 and 1879, apple exports from Pennsylvania and surrounding regions to Europe had quadrupled, and the Brits, in particular, grew to appreciate American varieties such as Baldwins, Northern Spy, and Newtown

VARIETIES BY MONTH

August Ginger Gold, Gala

September McIntosh, Jonathan, Red Delicious, Golden Delicious, Empire, Cortland, Jonagold

October Stayman/Winesap, Mutsu (Crispin), Rome, Nittany, Braeburn, York Imperial, Granny Smith, Fuji

Pippins. The expansion of commercial shipping via waterways and railroads encouraged the rapid growth of Pennsylvania's apple industry, as more efficient forms of transportation opened new markets for apples, both domestically and abroad. The discerning palates of the English demanded a wide range of varieties that grew best in Pennsylvania and the surrounding areas.

But just as commercial apple growers in the United States today fear the competitive threat of imports from countries such as China, so the English then feared apple imports from America and began a crusade to promote their own varieties. Commercial growers worked to identify the varieties most appropriate for Britain's climate and consumer preferences. English fruit growers had good reason to wring their hands and fret over their competitors across the ocean.

Though experts insisted that any variety grown in America also could be grown in the homeland soil, the truth was that certain varieties were less than desirable when attempts were made to cultivate them in the orchards of England. Added to this was the fact that American growers showed more single-minded dedication to cultivating high-quality apples of many varieties. Enterprising Colonial nurserymen provided carefully grafted trees that provided a good foundation for the commercial industry in America. The states, including Pennsylvania, sent beautiful, good-tasting Jonathans, Golden Russets, Grimes Goldens, and Winesaps across the seas.

Even within the United States, apples are distinctively different from one region of the country to another, especially when comparing western apples to those grown in the eastern states, including Pennsylvania. Washington State, in particular, has earned a reputation for apples that look perfect. For years, western pomologists worked toward developing apples with intense color and consistent shape distinctively characteristic of each variety. As a result of this controlled research and cultivation, the flavor of western-grown apples has suffered. Pennsylvania apples, on the other hand, though often not as colorful and perfectly shaped as Washington-grown apples, have retained a richer, more intense flavor.

Weather conditions also may contribute to regional flavor differences among apples. Some profess that Washington's soaking rains dilute the flavor of its apples compared with those grown in Pennsylvania's somewhat drier climate. Through sampling promotions, eastern apple marketers hope to encourage consumers to select apples based on taste and texture, rather than appearance.

As the apple business flourished throughout the United States, various regions of the country developed specific varieties most conducive to the climate and preferences of each area. The following are some of the varieties grown in Pennsylvania.

Braeburn

A chance seedling from New Zealand, the Braeburn is a newer variety and described as one of the firmest apples available. Most likely a descendant of the Granny Smith, the Braeburn is small to medium in size, with a somewhat oval shape. It is very crisp with a tart-sweet flavor, excellent for eating fresh or cooking. Braeburns are common to Pennsylvania's orchards.

Cortland

Although closely associated with an extensive breeding program that began in New York in 1895, the Cortland apple grows quite successfully in Pennsylvania. This red, midfall apple keeps fairly well. Mildly tart, it is a popular snacking apple but is also used in salads, applesauce, and for baking whole.

Empire

The Empire was named in honor of New York State, where it was developed by crossing a McIntosh and Red Delicious. With its mildly tart flavor and crisp, juicy texture, the dark red Empire is a quality dessert apple when eaten fresh. It is generally harvested in September and does well as a result of Pennsylvania's cool nights.

Fuji

As one might suspect from its name, the Fuji apple originated in Japan. Aromatic and somewhat crisp, the Fuji is an excellent dessert apple for eating out of hand and is growing in popularity today. It ranges in color from yellow-green to solid red.

Pennsylvania has been very successful in commercially growing Fuji apples for the fresh market.

Gala

Gala apples represent another contemporary favorite as a fresh-eating apple. A summer apple, the Gala has exceptional keeping qualities and a beautiful orange-red color on a creamy yellow background. The Gala's flesh is sweet, juicy, and crisp, and it is quickly gaining favor over the Red Delicious. As a result of the Gala's popularity, marketers have learned that consumers do care more about flavor and texture than a perfect, ruby red skin. Commercial planting of the Gala began in 1965 and spread quickly among American orchards, including several in Pennsylvania.

Ginger Gold

The Ginger Gold is Pennsylvania's early-summer apple–one of the season's first to reach farm markets and stores. This smooth, yellow apple is sweet and crisp and is a wonderful cooking apple. Discovered in 1979, the Ginger Gold is a relatively new variety with a short window of availability. Avid bakers would do well to seek out Ginger Gold as soon as it becomes available.

Golden Delicious

During the past few years, Golden Delicious apples have gained favor over Red Delicious in many parts of the country, as consumers enjoy their more complex flavor. Discovered in neighboring West Virginia in 1905, the Golden Delicious is suspected to be the pollen source for Pennsylvania's Nittany apple. Unlike the Red Delicious, which took more than a decade to gain popularity, the Golden Delicious apple caught on quickly and soon became a leading cultivar, not only in Pennsylvania, but across the United States and abroad.

Granny Smith

Like many commercial cultivars, the Granny Smith developed as a chance seedling. The apple was named after Maria Ann "Granny" Smith, an Australian who, in the 1860s, planted seeds from a Tasmanian cultivar called French Crab. Just one seed germinated, producing the tart, crisp, green fruit. Granny discovered the exceptional baking and keeping qualities of her find. It has become wildly popular around the world, and New Zealand is recognized as the first country to commercially market Granny Smiths.

The Grannies grown in Pennsylvania are recognized for their pink blush, uncommon to the versions from New Zealand and the western United States. Many consumers prefer the unique blush of Pennsylvania Grannies.

Jonagold

The Jonagold was introduced just two decades ago and is now grown all over the world. Developed in New York, the Jonagold was produced by conventional breeding methods crossing Golden Delicious and Jonathan varieties. Growers, including those in Pennsylvania, like the Jonagold because of its heavy yield, excellent eating quality, and large size. The variety is 30 to 80 percent red, and the remainder is somewhat golden yellow in color with touches of green. The flesh is soft yellow and semifirm, crisp, and unusually juicy. When the flesh is exposed to air, browning from oxidation develops slowly, making the apple popular for fresh slices. With its long shelf life, Jonagold is also conducive to processing applications. The variety prefers Pennsylvania's somewhat cool climate.

Jonathan

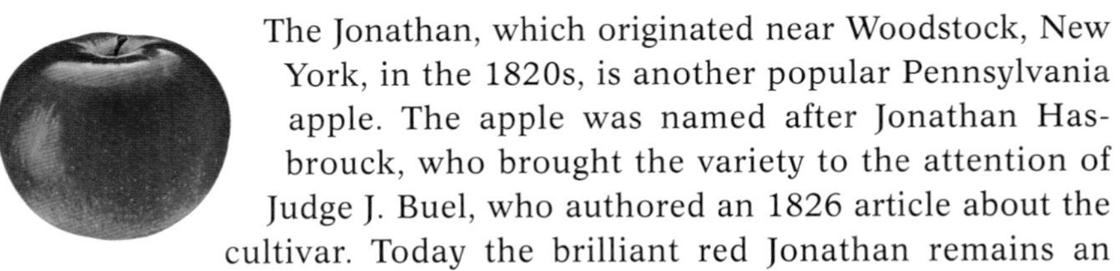

The Jonathan, which originated near Woodstock, New York, in the 1820s, is another popular Pennsylvania apple. The apple was named after Jonathan Hasbrouck, who brought the variety to the attention of Judge J. Buel, who authored an 1826 article about the cultivar. Today the brilliant red Jonathan remains an important commercial apple, as well as a popular eating and cooking apple. It grows best in the climates of Pennsylvania, Ohio, Virginia, Missouri, Arkansas, and irrigated regions out west. A few varietal synonyms for Jonathan include Ulster Seedling, Pomme Jonathan, Esopus, King Philip, and Philip Rick.

McIntosh

McIntosh represents another classic eastern apple. It was named after John McIntosh, the grower who discovered the variety on his Ontario, Canada, homestead in 1870. Like many other varieties, the McIntosh prefers the cool nights and clear days prevalent in Pennsylvania and other eastern states, as well as Canada. "Macs" are known for their sweet, strawberrylike flavor and white, juicy flesh.

Mutsu, or Crispin

The Mutsu, or Crispin, originated in Japan and is a cross between the Golden Delicious and a Japanese variety called Indo. In the United States, it grows best in the Appalachian region. This large, green apple with a yellow blush is an all-purpose apple that works well in pies and for applesauce.

Nittany

Another favorite Pennsylvania apple, the Nittany, was discovered by chance, as a randomly pollinated seedling of the York Imperial. Although the exact source of the pollination is not known, some researchers suspect it may have been the Golden Delicious apple. Named after its place of origin, Mount Nittany and its valley in Centre County, Pennsylvania, this apple may be favored partly due to its name association with the popular Penn State University Nittany Lions football team.

Although not grower-friendly, the Nittany apple has evolved from what many describe as a vigorous tree. The result is a great all-purpose apple with a tart, sweet flavor that makes it excellent for eating out of hand as well as for slicing into pies and cobblers. The Nittany has a color, flavor, and texture similar to the York and is generally oblong with a light cherry red coat.

Red Delicious

For years consumers looked to Washington State for one of the country's favorites, the Red Delicious. Today, however, improved strains throughout Pennsylvania have led apple enthusiasts to seek out the Keystone State's Red Delicious for its superior flavor. Many claim that the Pennsylvania Red is juicier and sweeter than its western counterpart. Although not as elongated as the Washington version, Pennsylvania's Red Delicious does have the characteristic, prominant calyx lobes on the bottom that make it easy to distinguish from other varieties.

Rome

With its characteristic red veins, the Rome, or Rome Beauty, originated in Rome Township, Ohio, in 1816. Pennsylvania's climate is much like Ohio's, and as a result, the Rome has become commercially popular in both states. Referred to as the "baker's buddy," the firm, tart Rome apples are especially good for baking or sautéing. Generally available starting in late October, Romes are excellent keepers.

Stayman/Winesap

Stayman/Winesap apples have a pleasing blend of sweet and tart flavors. Although the variety bore its first fruit in Kansas in 1875, it grows well in Pennsylvania and is quite popular, especially for its excellent performance in cooking and baking. Sometimes just called Stayman, this is an October apple with firm, juicy flesh.

York Imperial

Pennsylvania is credited with the development of the York Imperial cultivar, which dominated Appalachian fruit production for many years. York's origin dates back to the early 1800s, when either John Kline or a Mr. Johnson (depending on the source) spotted schoolboys raiding his Hellam Township, York County, orchard. After Kline chased away the boys, he noticed that under one tree, some apples had remained unusually firm and crisp even though they had fallen months before and lay buried under snow and leaves. He took samples of these apples to York nurseryman Jonathan Jessup, who grafted the York onto other rootstocks to ensure the future of the discovery. Later the new strain was propagated by John C. Schmidt, owner and operator of Springwood Farms in York County.

The York Imperial's exceptional keeping qualities explain its nineteenth-century popularity in northern Virginia and southern Pennsylvania, where growing conditions were ideal. The York dominated Appalachian fruit production for many years and was exported to European markets throughout the 1900s. As apple consumers in Europe and the United States became more discriminating, however, the York Imperial could no longer compete in the fresh market

York Apples—Pennsylvania's "Imperial" variety

with better-looking, deeper red counterparts such as the Red Delicious, and by 1930, the export market for Yorks, especially in England, had disappeared.

Processors recognized the York's benefits, however. The York was a firm, disease-resistant apple with a slightly yellow flesh, and its excellent color, texture, and keeping characteristics were desirable in producing good applesauce and canned slices for baking. When peeled and cored, the York apple produced high yields, another attribute appreciated by processors throughout the apple-producing regions of Pennsylvania, New York, and Virginia, who wished to maximize profits.

Today the York Imperial remains the preferred fruit of many processors, and many apple growers devote their orchards to Yorks to be used at one of several apple-processing plants in the area. The total production of Yorks is declining, however, and prices received for the fruit in the next few years no doubt will dictate its fate. Improved red strains, such as the Red Yorking and Commander York, could help the variety maintain its processing market dominance in Pennsylvania.

Heirloom Varieties

In addition to dozens of commercial varieties, many heirloom apples continue to be grown throughout Pennsylvania. Beginning in late August and well into early winter, the treasured but less-known varieties are available at farm markets and roadside stands.

Elstar. A cross between the Golden Delicious apple and a variety known as Ingrid Marie, this is a sweet-tart, firm, juicy apple that is very good eaten raw. The skin is a vibrant red, balanced with orange and yellow stripes.

Liberty. Similar in appearance and flavor to the McIntosh, the Liberty is more tart and crisp. It is a midseason apple and quite resistant to disease.

Lowry. Named after John Lowry, who discovered it on his Virginia farm in 1850, this variety is medium-sized and dark red, with faint white dots over the skin. Lowry is a crisp, juicy apple, at its peak in September.

Melrose. This variety is a cross between Jonathan and Red Delicious. The result is a greenish yellow apple with a soft brown blush. Melrose has a sweet, refreshing taste and crisp texture.

Northern Spy. This late-season variety has a yellow-green skin, red blush, and somewhat yellow flesh. Firm, with a balance of sweet and tart flavors, the Northern Spy is very well suited to cooking and processing.

Smokehouse. This red- and yellow-skinned variety has a mild but pleasant flavor. The Smokehouse is a late-season apple.

Spartan. A cross between the well-known McIntosh and the lesser-known Newtown Pippin, Spartans are good all-purpose eating and cooking apples. They have a sweet flavor, firm texture, and pure white flesh. Spartans are popular among cider makers.

Spencerville. This is a good-quality, sweet dessert apple, described as a cross between a McIntosh and a Golden Delicious. Its yellow skin is generally streaked with red and orange. Spencervilles keep very well.

Summer Rambo. This green and red apple is named for its early-season harvest. It is quite flavorful and juicy, and is suitable for baking and cooking.

Winter Banana. Large, golden-yellow, and firm, the Winter Banana often displays a pink blush. It is sweet, keeps well, and is good for cooking.

The Roots of

Pennsylvania's Apple Trees

Apples may be as old as mankind. Rustic etchings on cave walls and the remains of dried, ornamental apple rings discovered in ancient tombs indicate that apples predated recorded history by many centuries, as far back as the Iron and Stone Ages.

As long ago as five thousand years, the Chinese plucked apples from wild trees in the most remote areas of their homeland. They replanted the seeds, growing and cultivating domestic apples in their well-groomed gardens, and carried them to other parts of the world, initially Rome, Greece, and Persia. The first apples were as crisp, succulent, and flavorful as they are today, and these attributes led to the fruit's distribution across most parts of the Mediterranean some two thousand years later. Today some pomologists believe that the modern-day apple was the result of three varieties native to the Pyrenees in Europe crossed with the original variety.

First a symbol of wealth and status, apple orchards were the norm in the generously landscaped, walled courtyards surrounding the expansive Roman mansions of the rich. The Roman word for these gardens was *paradisus,* which later came to mean earthly paradise.

We all know the story of how Eve, tempted by the Serpent, persuaded Adam to eat the forbidden fruit in a paradise called the Garden of Eden. Although the Bible does not specify the fruit of temptation as an apple, artists have interpreted the story as such. The fifteenth-century Flemish artist Hugo van der Goes, for example, depicted Adam and Eve beneath an apple tree in his well-known painting *The Fall of Man.*

Apples were a symbol of love and fertility in many Greek and Roman stories, although there were few specific references to apples. Most of the stories referred to "round, fleshy fruit," which might have described quinces or pomegranates just as easily as apples. However, the apple is the only fruit with a species native to Greece, which makes a strong case for the apple's role in mythology.

In ancient Greek mythology, Zeus and Hera were married in the Garden of the Gods, where a tree bearing golden apples that tasted like honey and possessed mystical healing powers sprang from the earth.

The fall of Troy also was attributed, at least in part, to the apple. As explained in mythology, the Greek goddess of strife, Eris, was offended because she was excluded from the marriage celebration of Peleus and Thetis (the parents of the hero Achilles). In her rage, Eris threw a golden apple, inscribed with the words "To the Fairest," from her heavenly throne into the center of the wedding nuptials. The hurled apple was interpreted as a sign, a command that Paris, the son of the king of Troy, choose the fairest from among three goddesses who were present at the wedding. Paris chose Aphrodite, goddess of love, because she had promised him the hand of the world's most beautiful woman, Helen of Troy. Paris sailed to Sparta to find Helen, who, as fate would have it, was the wife of the Spartan king. Paris abducted Helen, and the result was the onset of the Trojan War.

With time, the apple was no longer an exotic fruit exclusively for the rich. Instead, apples had become accessible to the middle class when gardeners learned how to cultivate dwarf trees from the original apple-growing experts, the Chinese. Dwarf trees were created by grafting twigs or buds from the highest-quality apple trees onto young root systems from trees that would not grow much taller than the height of garden walls. Thousands of dwarf apple trees could be obtained from just one original tree.

As apple trees became the property of middle-class Europeans, growers began to experiment with different varieties. Farmers learned that the dozen or so individual seeds within one apple could be cultivated to produce different varieties. Various regions of Europe grew their favorite apples and those most conducive to the climate of their homeland. Apples had become the Old World's most popular fruit, not only because they tasted wonderful, but also because they kept well when stored in cool, dry surroundings.

Wild crab apples were native to the New World, but not until after 1492 did apples as we know them provide nutritious and satisfying food for travelers sailing to America. Pilgrims and pioneers not only ate the fruit, but also saved the seeds in anticipation of their own gar-

APPLE PHRASES AND DERIVATIVES

An apple a day keeps the doctor away. From an old English saying, "Ate an apfel avore gwain to bed makes the doctor beg his bread."

Apple eater. A term for one who is easily led astray, derived from the biblical story of the Garden of Eden.

Apple of his eye. This phrase is found throughout the Old Testament of the Bible and refers to God's regard for the Israelites.

Apple polisher. Term for an excessive flatterer coined in the 1920s and derived from the old tradition of an eager student who gives his or her teacher an apple.

Big Apple. Favored name for New York City popularized by jazz enthusiasts in the 1920s, who may have borrowed it from horse-racing slang, which referred to the racetracks in and around the city as the "big apple" tracks because of the big prize money that could be won.

It's better to give than receive. Derived from a fourteenth-century saying using apples symbolically, "Betere is appel y-yeue than y-ete." (Better is the apple you give than you get.)

One bad apple spoils the bunch. Based on a quote from Chaucer, "The rotten apple injures its neighbors."

Paradise. From the Persian word *pairidaeza,* a walled garden containing apple trees.

Pomology. The science of fruit growing, particularly apples. The word is derived from the name of the Greek goddess of fruit, Pomona.

Apples are promoted as nature's toothbrush in this vintage poster.

dens in the New World. The result was thousands of new apple varieties in America, and farmers became experts on what kinds grew best in various climates and soil types.

In Colonial America, apples were primarily used for making cider and applejack and for feeding livestock. By 1775, one in every ten New England farms included a cider mill. Applejack, the sweet, intoxicating version of cider, had become an important form of currency. It was used to pay for everything from medical services to a child's education, and it was served freely at breakfast and supper. As one Protestant minister described it, "The cider barrel was cherished far more than the apple bin."

Colonial cider making afforded opportunities for the legendary Johnny Appleseed, as well. The cider mills of western Pennsylvania provided many of the seeds he planted up and down the Ohio River in the early 1800s. Those Pennsylvania seeds made it to Wellsburg, West Virginia, where the eccentric Johnny founded a nursery with his brother. From there, he paddled farther down the Ohio River and hiked to central Ohio, where he handed out seeds to any settler who promised to plant and care for them. He also continued to plant seeds himself, but he seemed to enjoy engaging others in his serious hobby. Often traveling on foot, Johnny relied on a coarse sack to carry his apple seeds as far west as Indiana. Born Johnathan Chapman in 1744, he died in 1847, leaving a hundred thousand miles of plantings behind.

During the 1680s, Swedish colonists established the first known apple orchards in the New World along the Delaware River. By the 1800s, more than a thousand apple varieties were prevalent in America, and many of those were common to Pennsylvania. The state's Native Americans also cultivated their own apple and peach orchards, and tribes traded apples as if they were gold.

The entrepreneurial spirit of the colonists motivated them to not only grow apples for their own families, but also use them as a way to generate income. Apples were packed in barrels bound for London and Rome, where urban dwellers would pay well for the crisp, red "fruit of the gods." Benjamin Franklin, known as the "father of the American apple export business," shared a shipment of apples from his Philadelphia home with the British Court in 1759, further boosting apple exports from the colonies.

Many areas of the Keystone State have mountain slopes, which protect apple trees from biting wind and frost and provide drainage for the sandy, moist, and not-too-rich soil that apple trees prefer. All fruit trees require plenty of sunshine and cool nights, which are characteristic of Pennsylvania's Appalachian mountain ridges, especially in southern regions of the state. An appreciation for the art and science of growing apples drew many settlers to those parts of Pennsylvania where apple trees could thrive.

Franklin County

In 1771, some of the first permanent settlers in what is now the Scotland area of Franklin County were led by the Thompson family, with their twelve children. From Glasgow, Scotland, they named the settlement after their homeland. Although they loved their native country, it was ruled at the time by an oppressive government, which led them to migrate to America and Pennsylvania's rich farmland. Thompson named his six-hundred-acre plantation Corker Hill, and his sons went to work clearing the land for an apple orchard. With time, the Thompsons' apples gained a reputation for exceptional quality and abundance.

By the late 1800s, popular apple varieties in and around Scotland, Pennsylvania, included Hoops, Sheepnose, Vandevers, Romanites, Red Streaks, Grey House, Grind Stone, Queen, Old Horse, Dominie, Pippins, and Greenings. There were plenty of folks to pick the apples at that time, but only under certain conditions. It was commonly believed that unless apples were picked on the day of the full moon,

Local folks picked apples along Pennsylvania's North Mountain Fruit Belt to earn a living during the 1920s.

Workers prepare herbicides from scratch near Apple Way, Franklin County, Pennsylvania, 1920.

they would not keep well throughout the winter months, even when stored in the ultimate conditions offered by cool caves and cellars.

Scotland, and Franklin County in general, had become one of Pennsylvania's best apple-growing regions. That area was part of the appropriately named North Mountain Fruit Belt, which grew and harvested thousands of acres of apples every year. A thirty-mile stretch of dirt road called Apple Way ran right through the fruit belt and provided the area's commercial apple growers with the most accessible route to railway stations at Lehmasters and Fort Loudon. In 1931, area growers wrote a letter to Pennsylvania's secretary for the Department of Highways, requesting that Apple Way be upgraded for easier transportation of fruit. Now paved, Apple Way remains a scenic, apple-tree-lined road just off Route 30, north of Edenville. Throughout the state, including Franklin County, the commercial apple industry flourished with the expansion of the railroad, development of refrigerated cars, and improved roads. Today Franklin is second only to Adams among Pennsylvania counties in apple production, with more than 40 million pounds annually.

Adams County

Adams County also became a focal point of apple production in Pennsylvania. Quakers chose an area in what is now Butler Township as the first site in Adams County to grow apples commercially. The Quakers called their settlement Guernsey after the cow breed, although the area had been known previously as Sunnyside.

In the early years, Guernsey had a general store, warehouse, creamery, railroad station, and post office. In 1884, the tracks for the railroad connecting Gettysburg and Harrisburg were laid and ran through Guernsey. The town had its own station shop and sidetrack so that freight cars could be detached from the train and left for loading and unloading of goods, including apples.

In 1884, the Quakers built the Guernsey Bridge, a high, arched, wooden structure. William Tyson, C. Arthur Griest, and F. E. Griest were instrumental in building the bridge, which soon became important to commercial apple operations throughout the Quaker Valley. The bridge spanned the Gettysburg and Harrisburg Railroad, allowing farmers easy access from one orchard to the next, and beyond. Farm equipment was easily moved across the bridge and to trains for transporting where needed for apple production. During harvest, fresh apples were carted in barrels across the Guernsey Bridge, then shipped by rail to eastern seaports, from which they sailed to Europe.

In addition to its functionality, the bridge provided an impressive view of the nearby Quaker Valley Country Club, framed by apple orchards in every direction. During the 1930s, Reading Railroad workers maintained the Guernsey Bridge. Although it was dismantled in 2001 because of its poor condition, local preservationists hope to reconstruct it in the future.

By the early 1900s, Guernsey had become a popular gathering spot for growers wanting to buy apples, farm equipment, and feed. In 1920, Guernsey built its own social club, the Quaker Valley Country Club and Golf Course. Located west of town, the clubhouse was a converted creamery and served its members well. Most were attorneys and business owners from Gettysburg, who used the club to socialize and network. The club thrived until the Great Depression, when the golf course was returned to its original owner, and the clubhouse was converted to a private residence.

IMPERIAL TRAINS

"For the first time in my recollection, a train loaded entirely with apples was drawn out of our neighborhood. It went up hill and would not be counted a large train, as trains go, containing 15 cars, I think, but it was an apple train nevertheless. We expect this to become in the not-distant future an occurrence so common as to pass without comment, but it is worth mentioning now. We read frequently in the papers of cattle trains from Wyoming and Texas, ore and coal trains from Pennsylvania, watermelons or peaches from the south and vegetables from the Peninsula. Why not Imperial trains, York Imperial trains from Adams County?"

—Excerpt from the welcome address by Robert M. Eldon, president of The Fruit Growers Association of Adams County, in Fruit Growers Hall, Bendersville, Pennsylvania, December 18, 1907 (*Proceedings for the Year 1907).*

After 1900 and the evolution of settlements like Guernsey, commercial apple operations in the Keystone State quadrupled. Today there are more than three hundred commercial growers in Pennsylvania, and an equal number of smaller apple operations. Adams County is responsible for most of the state's apple production, generating more than 225 million pounds each year.

THE NATIONAL APPLE MUSEUM

The Biglerville Historical and Preservation Society was founded in 1981 by Jean and Marian Harbaugh, who saw the need to protect the history and heritage of Pennsylvania's apple industry. Biglerville was the most logical place to begin. Clair and Marie Ditzler donated their ninety-two-by-fifty-foot Sillik barn to the historical society as the location for the National Apple Museum. Hundreds of volunteers donated their time and energy to converting the pre–Civil War barn into a museum and filling it with wonderful artifacts important to Pennsylvania's apple industry.

The museum opened in April 1990. Exhibits include early orchard photographs and a walk-through display of farm equipment, including apple peelers, cider presses, and a vinegar generator. The museum houses plenty of authentic apple memorabilia and is open April through October of each year, Saturdays from 10 A.M. to 5 P.M., and Sundays from noon to 5 P.M. Tour guides are on duty, and group tours may be scheduled by appointment. There is a modest admission fee. Call 717-677-4556 for more information.

Biglerville

Biglerville, in Adams county, is the very heart and soul of Pennsylvania's apple country. Few other towns are mentioned as often in reference to the state's fruit industry, and an impressive list of growers lived in or around the original country village. In the early years, those local people called their community Sugartown, most likely because it was surrounded by acres of orchards bearing sweet fruit, not only apples, but peaches and cherries as well.

Prior to 1884, Biglerville could only be described as a rustic, primitive village. In 1863, at the time of the nearby battle of Gettysburg, Biglerville had twenty-four houses and businesses, most located east of the railroad. There were saddle and wagon makers, a hotel, justice of the peace, blacksmith shop, country store, marble works, and steam hub factory, as well as a one-room schoolhouse where students eagerly presented freshly picked, bright red apples to their teacher.

The town's face changed, however, with the growth of the railroad, and in 1903, Biglerville was incorporated as a borough. During the Depression era of the 1930s, farm wages ran 10 to 15 cents per hour, and fruit growers generally paid their workers $1 per day. Exceptional farmhands and their families were provided housing and land for

THE APPLE HARVEST FESTIVAL

On Sunday, October 14, 1961, Donald Trostel and Clair Fetters cochaired the first Apple Harvest Holiday in Adams County. The event included displays of both antique and modern farm equipment, fresh apples, apple dessert and cider booths, an apple butter boil, and meals of pancakes and sausages.

The Apple Harvest Holiday grew in popularity from one year to the next, and by 1965, it had evolved into the Adams County Apple Harvest Festival, sponsored by the Upper Adams Jaycees. The festival boasted an antique car display, apple cider press, apple butter boil, pony rides, bus tours of Apple Country, apple desserts, and sales of fresh apples and related products. A Pennsylvania Dutch–style meal was available, and there were ample commercial displays, a souvenir booth, and an appearance by the Apple Blossom Queen. Johnny Schmoker's German Band and the Cannonaiders Square Dancing Team provided entertainment.

Kids enjoy bobbing for apples at the National Apple Harvest Festival in Arendtsville.

In 1967, the festival became a three-day event and included tours of nearby apple-processing plants, an antiques flea market, helicopter rides, a display of antique steam engines, and a plethora of apple products. There was more entertainment than ever, including a movie called *The Miracle of Apples.*

In 1975, the Jaycees expanded the festival over the first two weekends in October, and today it is still held in Arendtsville, Pennsylvania. In 1977, the event was renamed the National Apple Harvest Festival, and indeed, it is the largest festival of its kind in the United States. For more information, contact the Adams County Fruit Growers Association at 717-677-7444.

Several other apple festivals are held in Pennsylvania. For a listing, see pages 83–86.

gardens and animals. Bushels of apples were awarded, as well, and considered a fringe benefit of the job. At that time, apples sold for $1 a bushel, including the basket they were packed in. Today Pennsylvania's fresh market apples sell for $8 to $15 per bushel, depending on grade and variety, and they are packed in nonreturnable corrugated boxes that usually display the name and logo of the packer.

Nowadays, travelers enjoy Biglerville for its quaint country store on the square, at the intersection of Routes 34 and 234, and many other reminders of a colorful past.

Pennsylvania

Apple Growers

Many of Pennsylvania's present-day apple growers have ancestors who migrated to the state in the 1800s and, like friends and family who settled before them, viewed the Appalachian Mountains as an opportunity to farm and prosper. When you talk to Pennsylvania's contemporary growers, you find that most can trace their families back at least three generations, and often further, when their ancestors first planted apple trees as a way to make a living and feed their families. There was something in the heart and blood of Pennsylvania's apple-growing pioneers that held fast through the twentieth century until today, when there remain more than three hundred serious commercial apple growers in the Keystone State.

Many Pennsylvania growers inherited their orchards from a parent. Sons and daughters continue to work the land and rely on their own children to help whenever possible. However, some offspring look toward college and careers as lawyers and doctors instead of apple growers.

It's amazing to find that there are Pennsylvania farm families, including apple growers, who are still virtually self-sufficient, though surrounded by bedroom community dwellers and white-collar workers who think that megacorporations own and operate all the country's farmland and that there are no small growers left.

In reality, a number of American farms, including many in Pennsylvania, continue to be owned and maintained by independent operators. They work impressive acreage, draw important income from their own farm markets, and continue to put in long days. Those days still begin before sunrise, and their agendas remain contingent upon the weather forecast.

Apple growers are a tired lot and extremely busy, especially during the months leading up to harvest. In spite of burdensome schedules, many are active members of their county, state, and national fruit-grower associations. Through "twilight" meetings and similar efforts, growers stay apprised of the latest government issues, farming technology, and concerns of their neighbors.

Pennsylvania growers appreciate the apple orchards passed down from their great-grandparents, and in spite of difficult economic times, most refuse to surrender their crops to suburban sprawl and the temptation to make what some would believe to be fast and easy money by "selling out" to developers. Instead, most growers steadfastly work through the cycles of apple production year after year, and though they may complain about the hard work and unpredictable weather, they feel that the options are unexplored and uncomfortable territory.

Pennsylvania's apple business is rich in history. There are so many families and communities who have influenced years of apple production within the state. That's why it's impossible to mention all of Pennsylvania's growers in a book of this scope. The following profiles represent a very small cross section of Pennsylvania apple entrepreneurs, their families, and businesses.

The art of apple picking has not changed much with time, although engines replaced horses in the orchard.

A horse-drawn chemical sprayer worked the orchards in the 1920s.

Strite's Orchards

Strite's Orchards is a classic example of the traditional apple-growing family business. Penn State graduates, business partners and brothers, Joe and Tom Strite, along with their wives and sons, quietly work 50 acres of apple trees and more than 220 additional acres of land devoted to agricultural products.

The Strite family has owned their land, located just off Route 322 between Harrisburg and Hershey, since 1843. Grandfather Joseph C. Strite planted his first apple trees in 1914, and shortly after, he quit his job on the railroad to begin selling fresh fruit at the Broad Street Market in downtown Harrisburg. At that time, there were few people near Strite's Orchards, and Joseph realized the need to take the product to his customers.

"We started out in the middle of nowhere," says grandson Joe. "Even in the early fifties, Strite's Road was dirt, with only one other house on it." Now most of Strite's Orchards are enveloped by homes and commercial enterprise. Surrounded by suburban sprawl, the Strites do well attracting the nearby concentration of customers, a loyal following who enjoy the short ride to Strite's farm market, located right on the orchards since the 1950s and rebuilt in 1994.

STRITE'S ORCHARDS

1000 Strite's Road
Harrisburg, PA 17111
717-564-3130
www.stritesorchard.com

Consumers have plenty of apple varieties to choose from at Strite's and look forward to the harvest of about 2.5 million apples annually, beginning with early-summer varieties like Lodi and continuing through the season until Granny Smiths are picked in October. The family sells all of its produce directly to consumers through the market and offers holiday gift baskets and boxes, as well as opportunities to "pick your own."

"We ship right from our market and also sell jelly, apple butter, sauce, and our own cider," says Tom Strite. "We like to offer a wide selection of fresh apple varieties and value-added products to keep our customers coming back."

The Strites coexist peacefully with their neighbors, are conscientious farmers, and refuse to sell their cherished land for development. The family enjoys agriculture and works year-round to continue a livelihood that is losing more and more ground, both literally and figuratively, every year.

Rice Fruit Company

Rice Fruit Company is a large, modern packer, shipper, and marketer of fresh apples located in Adams County, Pennsylvania. The company's current owners and operators are seventh-generation members of the apple-growing Rice family. The original ancestors, led by Daniel Reis, were German and settled in Adams County in the 1780s. They bought a five-hundred-acre farm on Potato Road from what was part of the original estate of William Penn. When Daniel Reis died, he willed the farm, which included a number of apple orchards, to his son, Henry. The will was explicit about providing specific amounts of farm staples to his wife, out of concern for her well-being. By this time, apples provided significant income to the Rice family and noticeably impacted the surrounding landscape.

RICE FRUIT COMPANY
2760 Carlisle Road
P.O. Box 66
Gardners, PA 17324
717-677-8131
www.ricefruit.com

In 1913, fifth-generation Arthur Rice Sr. founded the Rice Produce Business. He developed business enterprises in and around Biglerville, Chambersburg, Newport, Gettysburg, Orrtanna, and Franklin County. In the early years, Rice's primary business was packing apples in hundred-pound barrels, many of which were exported to England. York Imperials were well received by the English and constituted most of the apples shipped there at that time.

Arthur's younger brother, John, joined the business in 1921 after graduating from Gettysburg College. The enterprising John created an improved, more economical apple bushel basket with an expandable liner. This led to the development of a new company, Rice, Trew and Rice, in 1929. A production plant to make the new baskets and liners was built in Biglerville. At the time, the containers were more profitable than the apples.

After Arthur Rice Sr. died in 1941, his son, Arthur Jr., expanded Rice, Trew and Rice by establishing a new facility in southern Illinois. There, Arthur Jr. manufactured cushion pads for lidded fruit bushel and half-bushel baskets. The company's bushel baskets were replaced by corrugated boxes in 1946.

In 1954, Arthur Jr. sold his interest in Rice, Trew and Rice to his uncle and moved back to Adams County, where he rebuilt the Rice Produce Company into Rice Fruit Company. Located in Gardners, Rice remains a well-respected leader in the fruit industry today and packs fresh fruit for more than fifty growers located in Pennsylvania, Maryland, Virginia, and New York.

John Rice, who manages the business along with his three brothers, describes the scope of Rice Fruit Company: "Today, Rice Fruit Company packs over a million bushels of apples, peaches, pears, and nectarines, which are shipped to markets all over the eastern U.S. and Canada and to numerous markets overseas, especially Central and South America. We have even shipped apples to Saudi Arabia, Singapore, and Indonesia. It's the largest fresh apple–packing facility east of the Mississippi."

Shatzer Fruit Market

Shatzer Fruit Market is home to one of Franklin County's most involved and well-known apple-growing families. In 1933, Edison and Martha Dixon Shatzer moved to Martha's uncle's farm, and a year later, she began a small enterprise, selling eggs, jelly, and fruit from the yard. The farm included five hundred apple trees, and the Shatzers saw this as a business opportunity. In 1944, they purchased the farm that they had helped manage for so long and made plans to open a fruit market along the Lincoln Highway. By 1950, Shatzer Fruit Market was thriving, selling eggs, jelly, milk, and butter, in addition to apples, plums, and pears.

SHATZER FRUIT MARKET

2197 Lincoln Way West
Route 30
Chambersburg, PA 17201
717-263-2195

Shatzer Fruit Market, near Chambersburg, stands next to the original brick farmhouse where the family first sold its fruit from the front porch.

The Shatzers constructed a new farm market building, and by 1971, another generation of family members–Wilma Shatzer Mickey, her husband, Jack, and their son, Dwight–were successfully managing the orchard business and continue to do so today. Family members are immersed in state and local fruit associations and became master farmers in 1997. Wilma is particularly interested in the history of Franklin County's apple business and is quite hands-on in marketing the family's thirty acres of apples.

"Fruit demand has decreased a lot in the past ten years due to the changing lifestyles of consumers," says Wilma. "People don't cook and eat as much in the home, and therefore, much less fresh fruit is needed."

Much of the fruit grown today by the Mickey family goes to the Knouse Foods Cooperative, though fresh fruit is still available at the farm market on Route 30, Lincoln Way West, near Chambersburg.

Brown's Orchards and Farm Market

Accurately touted as having "a family tradition of freshness," Brown's Orchards and Farm Market are worth the trip through southern York County along the Old Susquehanna Trail, formerly the main route from Baltimore to Harrisburg and north. Near Loganville, the orchards include fifty acres devoted to apples, and the farm market has fruits and vegetables, a bakery, deli, gift baskets, candy, country gifts, sunroom, greenhouse, and ice cream stand. A wall-length mural depicting fruit orchards, rolling hills, and a farm frames the market's main display room. In 2001, York newspaper readers voted Brown's the "best local fruit and bakery."

Earl and Margaret Brown bought a thirty-five-acre fruit and poultry farm from relatives when the York Safe and Lock Company closed in 1948 and Earl lost his foreman's job. The family moved from the "big city" of York to the country town of Loganville, where they became farmers.

BROWN'S ORCHARDS AND FARM MARKET

300 South Main St.
Loganville, PA 17342
717-428-2036
www.jarrettsville.org/family/browns.htm

In the late 1940s, the Brown family ran a modest roadside fruit stand some six hundred feet from where the current market is located. Although two of Earl's sons, Roger and Richard, left the farm for dentistry and banking, son Stan and his wife, Nona, stayed involved in the business. Their efforts contributed to the evolution of the existing market, with the encouragement of their oldest son, Scott. Nowadays, family members Brenda, Mandy, and Travis also help run the thriving operation.

Brown's represents four generations of family members who are "in their element" when working the orchard and market. Stan, now in his midsixties, and Nona continue to walk through the store almost every day, chatting with employees and answering customer questions about which apples make the best sauce, pies, and such.

Brown's Orchards and Farm Market draws visitors year-round.

"A trip to Brown's Orchards and Farm Market is like a visit with an old friend," states the website. "The family-like atmosphere is warm and inviting, and the market is filled with a wonderful display of country collectibles. And don't miss the home-made apple butter. That, alone, is worth a trip from just about anywhere."

Linvilla Orchards

Pennsylvania's Delaware Valley is home to a priceless treasure, the three-hundred-acre Linvilla Orchards. Owner-operators include several members of the Linvill family. They inherited a rich heritage from grandfather Arthur Linvill and his mother, who in 1914 bought "the farm with the octagonal barn."

At the time, Linvilla Orchards was used as a dairy farm, and the eighty-foot-wide, eighty-foot-high barn housed a herd of forty dairy cows. The barn, built in 1880, provided unique, efficient room and board for the cows as they stood around its perimeter, facing inward and eating and drinking from the center of the room.

Arthur Linvill also grew apple trees and drove his horse and wagon through the nearby communities to sell his harvest. Soon customers started going directly to the Linvill farm to buy fresh apples, and even today, longtime customers reminisce about the days when they purchased fruit right from Arthur's front porch.

The octagonal barn and farm market on Linvilla Orchards

Today third- and fourth-generation Linvills, including Steve and sisters Nancy, Susan, and Jean, continue to sell fresh vegetables and fruits, including apples, from the floor of the octagonal barn. The market features a complete line of produce, including about twenty-five varieties of apples (the Honey Crisp has been a favorite for the past few years), freshly pressed cider, apple butter, and bakery items brimming with fresh, spicy slices of fruit. Charming gift baskets filled with fresh apples and other fruit are creatively packed and shipped just about anywhere in the United States.

LINVILLA ORCHARDS

137 West Knowlton Road
Media, PA 19063
610-876-7116
www.linvilla.com

One of the last working farms in the Delaware Valley, Linvilla offers plenty of opportunities to pick your own apples from the orchards surrounding the family's unusual barn. By following the farm's harvest schedule, available on-line, you can treat your family to harvest-fresh apples. The orchard also offers many activities, including educational tours, hay rides, and swimming; a gift shop; and recipe ideas.

The family business is deeply rooted in Pennsylvania's Delaware Valley. "The first Linvills came to Pennsylvania in 1683 and settled near Upland, about three miles down the creek from Linvilla Orchards," explains Steve Linvill. "We laugh about the fact that the family has gotten only three miles in more than three hundred years."

Sixteen members of the Linvill family continue to live on the property and work in various aspects of the business. "We go to bed thinking about the farm and we wake up thinking about the farm," says sister Susan Linvill Jochum. "We never go home, because the farm is home."

Pennsylvania

Apple Production

The apple has remarkable adaptability and stamina in a range of temperatures and soils, and varieties have been grafted to tolerate climates once thought to show little promise for growing apples under any circumstances. Early Pennsylvania settlers recognized the adaptability and resultant financial potential of the apple tree in their own backyards. They experimented with well-known and lesser-known varieties until they had discovered which were most conducive for personal use and profit, often beyond the boundaries of the state.

Apple growers enjoy Pennsylvania's change of seasons and the challenges each presents. They have a strong sense regarding the optimum times for planting, cultivating, and harvesting, acquired through experience and possibly heredity. This allows growers to effectively manage their orchards, at least to the extent possible in the face of unpredictable Mother Nature.

Pennsylvania's most sought-after growers are those successful at cultivating the near-perfect apple, at least when doing so is within their control. Sometimes nature, personal health, or even government regulation has deterred fruit farmers from growing the ultimate apple. If conditions are right, however, commercial growers produce acres of trees that bear wonderful fruit worthy of display and judging at shows such as the annual State Farm Show and Exposition in Harrisburg. For many growers, winning the show's Best Bushel award is the highest honor, defining fall's ultimate harvest.

Apples receiving the Best Bushel award are displayed at the Farm Show in Harrisburg.

Growers remember each harvest and measure the current crop against those from previous years. When the apples are large and beautiful, approaching optimum size, flavor, and texture, they most likely will sell on the fresh market. Fruit that is smaller or weather-damaged is usually trucked to a nearby processing plant to be used for juice, sauce, and pie filling.

In recent years, production has been higher than consumer demand, and apple prices have been somewhat weak. However, growers have newfound optimism about the prices they will receive for their apples, because recent research about the fruit's nutritional benefits could help boost consumption, and efforts to keep foreign apples out of the United States have been successful, at least for the short term.

New generations of consumers often fail to appreciate the growers' efforts spent digging, pruning, measuring, planting, and worrying about every season's fruit crop. The plentiful, snowy blossoms and king, or most prominent, bloom on spring's apple trees promise a good harvest, but there are many corners to turn until fall. Will an overzealous government ban another pesticide never proven harmful to humans? Will another hailstorm destroy what was, just minutes before, perfect fruit? Will growers find the laborers necessary to harvest their fruit? Will consumers want at least as many apples and the same varieties as last year?

Apple consumption patterns in the United States make profits difficult. Commercial growers explain that the American consumer enjoys an occasional apple, but also appreciates an extensive variety of fresh, often exotic, produce alternatives. Consumers aren't baking and cooking from scratch as much as in previous decades, and the five or six apples that once went into a fresh pie now remain on the grocery shelf, sometimes beyond their intended life expectancy.

Pennsylvania's commercial apple industry also faces the threat of competition from the western United States and other countries, China in particular. Many growers are thankful for the additional and substantial income they draw from other businesses such as contracting or accounting, as these days, few rely solely on apple sales as a source of income.

Recently, growers throughout the country, including Pennsylvania, took advantage of federal market loss assistance, a cash payment to help bolster commercial apple businesses through difficult economic times. Most apple growers do not want to collect permanent, federally mandated payments along the lines of those received by grain farmers, though several agree that something needs to be done or many growers will go out of business. Today's profit seems to be quickly eaten up by equipment breakdowns, knee-jerk regulations, and lack of demand, all of which have resulted in irreversible damage to a once profitable business.

Apples are grown in all of Pennsylvania's sixty-seven counties. Adams, Franklin, York, and Cumberland Counties produce about two-thirds of the state's apples, and Bedford, Berks, Erie, Juniata, Lehigh, and Snyder Counties are close behind.

Pennsylvania is one of thirty-five states providing ideal conditions for growing apples commercially. On average, Pennsylvania produces 10 to 12 million bushels annually and ranks fifth among apple-producing states. Only Washington, Michigan, New York, and California produce more.

Apple trees cannot thrive in climates that remain too warm all year round; they need thirty to sixty days of chill to shed their leaves and rest during the winter. The state's southern counties, with their warm, clear days, cool nights, and adequate rainfall, are ideal for growing apples. The Appalachian foothills provide ample drainage and warming air, which circulates to protect the precious fruit trees from the biting cold and wintry frost that can linger well into spring.

Although most apple harvesting in Pennsylvania begins in late August, the management and maintenance of the orchard is a year-round proposition. Equipment must be repainted, storage facilities cleaned, and potential markets identified.

In the calendar year, pruning begins midwinter and runs through March. Each tree must be pruned to allow plenty of sunlight to reach

Pennsylvania's climate is perfect for orchards and apple-growing.

the innermost branches, ensuring the best opportunity for growth and quality fruit. Pruning is a labor-intensive art as much as it is a measured science.

Tree-planting and fertilization begin in April, with follow-up fertilization when the fruit is beginning to grow and, as a result, requires its greatest amount of nourishment. Compost or organic matter is often used as fertilizer.

Mowing begins in April as well. Modest amounts of grass, clover, or other ground cover are grown in the orchard to help prevent erosion and to retain moisture in the soil. Ground cover also helps boost organic composition. If cover grows too high or too thick, however, it can pull away moisture and nutrients from the trees and may attract insects. So growers cut the ground cover periodically throughout the year, often well into September.

Pesticide application, called Integrated Pest Management (IPM), also begins in April, and conservative spraying is done in carefully measured amounts to ensure apples that are both beautiful and safe. The final spraying is usually carried out from one to three months before the apples are ripe and ready for picking.

Pennsylvania's apple growers inspect the blossoms on their trees starting each spring. In the first stages, the blossoms are tightly closed and a gentle pink color. As spring unfolds, the blossoms open and turn soft white. At their peak, the blossoming trees are beautiful beyond description and look as if a late-winter snow had passed through the Appalachians on its way up the eastern shore.

Growers can tell a lot from the blossoming apple trees. A heavy amount of blossoms, called a "snowball bloom," signals an overabundance of small apples. In this case, growers will thin the blossoms in June and July, either by hand or by using a conservative amount of chemical to cause some of the blossoms to fall away from the trees. Workers are careful to avoid picking the largest flowers, called king blooms, because these will produce the largest fruit. The result is fewer blossoms and therefore larger apples, which often show more promise for the fresh apple market.

Summertime also brings concerns about moisture. If rainfall is adequate, the apples will grow and ripen on schedule. In recent years, however, droughts have forced Pennsylvania's commercial apple growers to rely on irrigation to ensure a healthy crop.

In summer, apple trees are cross-pollinated. Most cannot produce fruit from the pollen of trees bearing the same variety, and as a result, they must be cross-pollinated. Honeybees are most commonly used to pollinate apple trees, and growers often place bee colonies right in the orchards to ensure effective results.

Toward fall, growers remove foliage from the trees in an effort to minimize shadows on the fruit. Shadows prevent adequate sunlight from reaching the fruit, and without it, apples will not turn their classic red or multicolors. Workers may gently turn the apples so that all sides are exposed to sunlight over a period of weeks. In addition, workers may cut off unwanted branches and may prop or suspend branches to prevent them from sagging under the weight of several large apples.

Harvesting generally begins in late July or August, depending on the variety. Apples picked during this time are considered early apples by most eastern standards. Larger apple trees require four to six years to bear fruit, and the currently popular dwarf trees begin bearing apples in two to three years. Growers prefer the smaller trees because they can plant more per acre with maximum results. The average apple tree is productive for thirty to forty years or longer, if properly nurtured.

For fresh market apples, workers pick the fruit one at a time to prevent bruising. They place them in special canvas bags with openings at the bottoms that stay closed until the bags are full. Then pickers open the bottoms and carefully empty the apples into large wooden or plastic bins placed throughout the orchards. Some growers harvest the

Pennsylvania apples are still picked by hand.

Apple-picking ladders refuse to outlive their usefulness.

A worker releases freshly picked Pennsylvania apples from canvas bags.

Wooden bins full of Pennsylvania apples wait to be transported to the packing house.

apples mechanically if they are to be sold for processing, but many still opt to handpick, regardless of destination.

After the apples are picked, tractors and forklifts carry full bins to packing houses, where the fruit is presorted. Human hands remove leaves and any apples with visual defects. The apples that survive the presort are dumped into water tanks, where they pass along rubber conveyor belts to be sorted by size and quality. A catwalk allows onlookers to watch as the apples float to their various destinations to be packed in trays and bags. Although apples produce a natural wax that protects the fruit and helps in retaining moisture, many packers also polish them with a thin coating of harmless, edible wax to enhance their appearance. Large packing houses rely on computers to judge the quality of the fruit and determine its fate as fancy, extrafancy, or some other category, before being boxed.

Smaller apples are usually packed in three-, five-, or ten-pound bags. Larger apples that will be sold individually at the retail site are

Bins brimming with apples arrive at Pennsylvania packing houses each fall.

Apples are sorted by size and quality at the packing house.

Sorted apples float to their various destinations for packing in trays and bags, then boxes.

Only the best and the brightest make the grade.

KLEINFELTER APPLE BARRELS

Pennsylvania's early apple production relied on classic wooden barrels for storage and transport. Kleinfelter apple barrels were known for their functionality during the early 1900s and in the 1920s were the primary method of carrying apples overseas.

Each barrel could hold three bushels of apples. The barrel heads were made of pine from Alabama, the staves from Virginian gum or cottonwood, and the hoops from Arkansas elm. Raw materials came into Biglerville by rail, where they were manufactured into sturdy, reliable containers.

Apples were shipped in wooden barrels made in the heart of Pennsylvania's apple country, 1920s.

By 1930, Kleinfelter was manufacturing more than ninety-five thousand barrels for Adams, York, and Lebanon County apple growers. This was a challenging accomplishment, complicated by the fact that storage was scarce and deliveries were made by horse-drawn wagons. As a result, barrels were stored all over town, and the company purchased a 1925 Reo Speedwagon to facilitate deliveries and fill orders in a timely fashion. Around that same time, Kleinfelter purchased a fruit tree–spraying equipment franchise from a New York company and found that this enterprise rounded out the existing barrel production business.

By the mid-1930s, the new technology of bushel boxes and baskets was gaining favor over wooden barrels for holding apples, and the barrel-manufacturing business was on the decline. Kleinfelter entered the bushel box business but did not find it profitable. By 1943, the company was making only ten thousand barrels as a result of alternative packaging and the end of the apple export business during World War II. Despite efforts to augment the company's profits, Kleinfelter's barrel-making enterprise eventually dissolved and was replaced by an Allis-Chalmers tractor franchise.

Early, engine-powered wagons hauled apples (and peaches) in barrels to market.

packed in cardboard trays, which are stacked inside boxes. The boxes hold forty-eight to one hundred apples, depending on fruit girth. Traditional boxes weigh about forty-two pounds, although newer models weigh less. Some of the packed boxes are loaded onto pallets, then trucks for distribution. Packers prefer to sell their apples to retailers by the truckload, about one thousand boxes each.

Any remaining apples are placed in storage until ready to be shipped out to fresh markets. Growers used to rely solely on cool temperatures to help maintain apples in storage, but today many hold apples in sealed rooms with controlled atmospheres, called CA storage. Since apples continue to respire, or breathe, long after harvesting, they use oxygen and give off carbon dioxide. Although this once created soft apples over time, packers can now reduce the oxygen in their CA rooms to help minimize deterioration. Oxygen is forced out of the CA rooms, while carbon dioxide and nitrogen levels are increased. The apples are held at thirty-one degrees and maintain their quality for months, until ready for the production line or fresh market. (Because of their high sugar content, apples will not freeze until exposed to a temperature of twenty-eight and a half degrees.) Smaller packing houses have little, if any, storage and welcome the end of the supply long before the next harvest begins.

About 25 to 30 percent of Pennsylvania's apples are sold on the fresh market, either directly to consumers through farm markets and

Cardboard boxes eventually replaced wooden barrels for shipping apples

About 25 to 30 percent of Pennsylvania's apples are sold on the fresh market.

roadside stands, or via grocery stores virtually anywhere in the eastern United States. The remaining 70 to 75 percent go to nearby processing plants, such as the cooperative Knouse Foods.

Knouse Foods Cooperative

In the late 1800s, brothers John and Henry Mertz moved to Adams County, Pennsylvania, from New York and built two small fruit-processing plants, one in Bendersville and another in Biglerville. The Mertz brothers employed about twenty-five men and women to trim and peel apples, primarily the York Imperial, to be dried in coke-fired furnaces, then shipped to domestic and international markets.

In 1938, the Bendersville plant burned down, but the Biglerville facility ran until 1940, when C. H. Musselman purchased the plant and used it to dry apple pomace, the crushed pulp of the fruit. Musselman had a keen interest in apple processing and had already purchased another fruit-processing operation, the Biglerville Canning Company.

By 1912, canning had proven successful at the Biglerville location, and as a result, Musselman built a second plant to the north in Gardners, Pennsylvania. Workers peeled, trimmed, and quartered the fresh apples, then placed them in gallon cans. Six filled cans were packed in a wooden case, and the finished product was stored in barns, sheds, and warehouses until ready for market. Horse-drawn wagons transported the processed apples to market.

Not too many years later, a prominent fruit grower named William S. Adams built a small canning plant at Peach Glen, Pennsylvania, as an outlet for apples and vegetables provided by several area growers. Peach Glen is located in Adams County, the largest apple-producing county in the state. The United Grocery Company of Harrisburg purchased the plant a few years later, and under good management, production doubled every year for another decade. The plant was named the Knouse and Fohl Canning Plant, for the partners who owned it, and after Albert Fohl retired, it was renamed the Knouse Processing Plant. Meanwhile, Musselman continued to build and acquire businesses, including fruit farms, to advance his food processing empire.

In the 1940s, the Peach Glen Knouse plant was enlarged in order to supply processed products to the troops during World War II.

THE FRUIT RESEARCH LABORATORY

Established by the Pennsylvania State College (now Pennsylvania State University) in Arendtsville in 1918, the Fruit Research Laboratory originally was located in the Arendtsville Hotel. Two staff scientists were appointed to study pest problems that were important to fruit growers throughout the state. Chester Tyson, a fruit grower and member of the Pennsylvania State College Board of Trustees, was most influential in establishing the lab.

In 1922, the lab moved to the Arendtsville schoolhouse, in 1948, it found a home on East Main Street. In 1971, C. H. and Emma G. Musselman, founders of the Musselman Foundation, contributed $350,000 in funds, later matched by the state of Pennsylvania, to build a new fruit research facility among the rolling orchards near Biglerville. The lab continues its important research today and has contributed immensely to Pennsylvania's apple industry, especially in areas of integrated pesticide management, plant pathology, and horticulture.

Throughout the year, scientists study and solve problems associated with apple growth and production in the laboratory setting. The results are then tested in nearby orchards. Through group meetings and one-on-one instruction with growers throughout the state, the lab's researchers have helped Pennsylvania apple producers optimize the quality of their product. Today, Penn State's Fruit Research Laboratory is one of the most well respected in the country.

A display of the Knouse Foods product line.

Owner Milton E. Knouse was having some difficulty finding enough fruit for processing and, to solve the problem, bought several fruit farms to support his expanding enterprise.

By 1946, M. E. Knouse owned one of four apple-processing businesses located in Adams County. The other three were the Mann Brothers' Adams Apple plant in Aspers, the C. H. Musselman plants in Gardners and Biglerville, and the Ivan Z. Musselman plant in Orrtanna.

The processed apple industry was growing and thriving, which led to the formation of cooperatives. Co-ops consisted of growers who had a common ownership and interest in providing themselves with a needed service. Apple cooperatives meant that their members would share in the profits and losses of the business, considered a small risk in light of the benefits of having an outlet for their produce.

The PenMar VA Packers Cooperative had 260 grower members, and its president was Milton Knouse. Under his direction, the stockholders authorized their board of directors to purchase fruit-processing plants in Scotland, Chambersburg, and Peach Glen, and in Orrtanna, the Orrtanna Canning Company owned by Ivan Musselman. By 1950, the cooperative changed its name to Knouse Foods Cooperative, Inc.

Today, Knouse Foods remains a leader in producing applesauce and juice, pie filling, cider vinegar, and some four hundred other fruit products, many recognized as staples in the American kitchen. Knouse operates eight plants in four states, five of which are in Pennsylvania. Although Knouse buys some apples from other states, most are supplied by the approximately 130 growers who own the Knouse cooperative. Knouse processes other fruit, but apples are by far the primary product line. More than 8 million bushels of apples find their way to the Knouse facilities each year.

As the harvest builds throughout September, so does production at Knouse Foods. Truckloads of apples stacked in twenty-five-bushel bins arrive at the production house and are first inspected for imperfections, then weighed and unloaded. The best-quality fruit and earliest varieties go into CA storage. For more immediate use, the rest of the apples are held in a regular cold storage facility at about thirty-two degrees with high humidity.

Apples are inspected, washed, culled, and sorted for size, then transported by water flume to the production floor. Although Golden Delicious is considered a premium production apple, many other varieties, including York Imperial, Rome, Stayman/Winesap, and Red Delicious, are blended in different ratios, depending on the product to be made, to achieve the right product appearance, flavor, and texture.

Just prior to cooking, the apples are automatically peeled, cored, and sliced, then sent on to massive steam kettles and presses used to create sauce, juice, and pie filling. Cans and bottles are sealed, labeled, and randomly checked for quality, then shipped out to warehouses, where the product is held until sold for retail and food service markets. Knouse packs under various labels, including Lucky Leaf, Musselman's, Apple Time, Lincoln, and Speas Farms.

Adams County Fruit Packing and Distributing Company

The history of the Adams County Fruit Packing and Distributing Company truly is indicative of Pennsylvania's tightly woven apple tapestry. In 1911, the Biglerville Cold Storage Company was formed in Biglerville, Pennsylvania, and a year later, the company's storage building was completed, holding thirty-five thousand barrels of apples.

The company built its first central packing house in 1915 and was set up to brush, grade, and pack apples for distribution, not only within the United States, but to foreign markets as well. During the next decade, the company expanded, adding an office, factory, and warehouse where wooden apple barrels were made. The company was doing well and expanded again in 1923 to include the production of lime sulfur, a fungicide used on apple trees. In just a few years, the company had seventy-five thousand barrels of apples in storage, each barrel holding three bushels.

Adams County Fruit Packing changed hands several times during the next four decades, and in 1966, a familiar name in apple processing, the Musselman Company, purchased the cold storage facility. Years later, Knouse Foods purchased the facility from Musselman.

Over the years, the company's storage barrels were replaced by bulk bins, and cardboard boxes replaced bushel baskets. The storage facility remains in operation today.

Apples in

Food and Drink

Although nothing may equal the flavor of a crisp, fresh apple right from the tree, it didn't take Europe long, especially Italy and France, to use apples in cooking, especially in preserving and baking. The oldest apple recipe on record is Diced Pork and Matian Apples, a combination of pork and apples seasoned with coriander and honey. The creation comes from a third-century Roman cookbook called *De Re Coquinaria* ("On Cookery"), written by Apicius.

Although apples were used in cooking for centuries, the pace quickened once sugar made its way to Europe. Apples were cooked in the wonderful sweetener and preserved for the winter months. Sugar cookery offered seemingly endless possibilities for apple tarts, confections, and conserves, as well as preserves.

In the eighteenth century England had a sweet tooth. Puddings were the preferred medium for eating apples. At that time, more sugar was consumed in England than in France and this resulted in some delicious and inventive ways for the Brits to enjoy apples. In addition to English apple puddings, rich apple custards, and thick marmalades, robust tarts were fashionable and considered prestigious.

By the time America had gained its independence in 1776, apple orchards and cooking techniques were well established throughout the colonies, including Pennsylvania. The Keystone State's Swedish, Dutch, British, German, and Swiss immigrants melded their culinary talents to create new apple recipes in what some have described as a combination apothecary shop, brew house, and kitchen.

Pennsylvania's long winters demanded hearty, warm dishes, and Colonial apple pudding was one result. Fresh ingredients such as cranberries, pumpkins, and maple syrup encouraged experimentation and added dimension to the classic English version of the delicious dessert.

Although apple puddings remained popular throughout the colonies, it was apple pie, probably developed in the early 1700s, that became a symbol of patriotism. The earliest pies included the whole apple–core, peel, and all–and when fresh apples were not in season, dried apples were used to ensure that the pie was available year-round. Made in quantity, the pies fared well when kept outside during the subzero winters until eaten for breakfast or supper.

Pennsylvania Dutch Foods

German and Swiss emigrants came to America in the 1600s and 1700s to escape religious persecution in their homeland. By 1790, these groups and their descendants, known as the Pennsylvania Dutch, constituted about one-third of Pennsylvania's population. This led to their strong influence on the state's culinary traditions, and apples in many forms were an important part of the Pennsylvania Dutch diet.

The Pennsylvania Dutch took pride in their apple orchards and cultivated many varieties, including Smokehouse, Maiden's Blush, Rambo, Bellflower, Vandevere, Mama Beam, Fanny, Winter Banana, Hiester, Susan's Spice, Evening Party, Blue Mountain, Fallowater, Smith's Cider, and Pennsylvania's own York Imperial.

The women were known for their proficiency in preserving fruit in the form of jams and spreads, and apple butter was a favorite. When berries gave way to apple season, apple butter boils afforded women the opportunity to socialize while preparing one of the many "sweets and sours" so customary in the German diet.

Lotwarrick, or apple butter, was prepared in the farm's summer kitchen or outdoors in good weather. A huge copper kettle hung over the fire and held bushels of peeled apples and gallons of cider, the raw ingredients for apple butter. The mixture was stirred constantly over the open flame until thick and dark brown, then spooned into earthen crocks. The spread had excellent keeping qualities and lasted until the new apple harvest came around.

The Pennsylvania Dutch were also skilled at making applesauce and cider, which then became ingredients used to complement the flavor and texture of main dishes, side dishes, and desserts. In early fall, cider was stored alongside elderberry and dandelion wine until it could be sold, used to make apple butter, or stored in barrels to become vinegar.

Harsh winters prompted the Pennsylvania Dutch to become proficient at drying apples so that the fruit could be used any time of year for dumplings, fritters, and grunts (a type of cobbler), as well as in pies. They were sophisticated enough to sort and dry sweet and tart apple varieties for use in dishes most conducive to one flavor or another. Apple slices, with the peel still intact, were strung up in the kitchen or placed in a Dutch oven to dry before snowstorms rolled over the Appalachian Mountains. The Pennsylvania Dutch called their precious dried apples *Schnitz*, from the German word for "cut."

DRYING APPLES

Wash and dry desired number of red, green, or yellow apples. Core, then cut unpeeled apples into 1/4-inch-thick slices. Soak a few minutes in equal parts lemon juice and water. Drain on paper towels and pat dry. To dry in a conventional oven, arrange in single layer, and without touching, on baking sheets lined with waxed or parchment paper. Place in a 200-degree oven with door slightly ajar, and let dry 6 to 10 hours, turning slices a few times. To dry in a microwave, arrange about twenty rings at a time, in a single layer and without touching, on parchment paper or fresh paper towels. Microwave on defrost setting for 35 to 45 minutes, or until dry. Store dried apples in airtight container until ready to use for snacking or decorating.

Water or cider was used to rehydrate the apples. One story describes how an industrious Pennsylvania farmer accidentally dumped a wagon full of dried apples in a creek. As legend has it, the apples in the creek bed swelled so much that the valley flooded. As a result, the area was named Schnitz Creek.

Dishes were created around the plumped, rehydrated fruit. One popular dish was Schnitz un Knepp, sweet apples cooked with pork or ham and served with dumplings (see recipe on page 60). Pork and apples were a popular recipe combination for Pennsylvania's settlers. Cooks discovered that the apples helped reduce the fatty flavor and mouth feel of pork, and cured pork went well with apples throughout the long winter season.

George Washington loved Pennsylvania Dutch cooking and hired a German cook to feed his troops while stationed at Valley Forge. Washington and his soldiers favored schnitz pie. Schnitz are still made and sold commercially in mom-and-pop stores throughout Lancaster County and other parts of Pennsylvania Dutch country.

Cider

Connoisseurs of cider understand that the quality of the drink can vary, depending on how it is made and the variety of apples used. Generally, a blend of sweet and tart apples works best. Cider makers tend to keep their custom blends family secrets, passing them from one generation to the next by word of mouth, never writing them down for fear that they might be stolen by an enterprising competitor.

Cider was popular through history and made in all parts of the world as long as people have enoyed apples. The Greeks, Celts, and Romans prepared fermented apple drinks, which became a formidable competitor to wine. Cider could be clean and refreshing or rustic and lingering, depending on the methods and kinds of apples used.

Early cider-making methods involved piling ripe apples into a hollow tree trunk. The fruit was beaten and crushed to a pulp, releasing the juice, then left to ferment. This process was popular in England and was used well into the seventeenth century, especially in monasteries, where monks planted seedling orchards and applied their wine-making skills to apple juice.

Another cider-making technique, preferred by the French, involved brewing apple pieces in water, then fermenting the mix to create a popular alcoholic beverage. Later, mills and presses were developed to extract the juice from apples, and this advanced technology lead to more consistent quality and commercialization throughout Europe.

England's enthusiasm for fermented cider, in particular, spilled over into the New World. In Colonial times, any reference to the apple beverage was synonymous with the fermented version–hard cider. Early American settlers relied on fermented cider as their most favored drink. Many proclaimed their preference for hard cider out of concern for the quality of the water available to them. Historians record these early concerns about water as misplaced and possibly an excuse to indulge in an alcoholic beverage that was relatively easy to prepare.

By 1775, one in every ten farms in New England included a cider mill. Cider was used as currency to pay for schooling, repairs, and medication, and as a result, it played a central role in the economy of Colonial America. Cider was the beverage of choice and often started the farmer on his day. Physicians recommended the beverage for health, and cooks used cider vinegar to pickle vegetables and fruits.

Since wine grapes didn't fare well in all parts of the colonies, fermented cider became a fine substitute for wine. Children as well as

Cider-making in the 1850s.

adults drank hard cider and appreciated the beverage for its warmth and comfort, especially through the seemingly endless gray days of winter.

Colonists discovered that cider could also be distilled to make a brandy, which they called applejack. The American cider brandy was popular through the early nineteenth century. Well-to-do Colonial households owned copper stills for making fruit brandies, and commercial distilleries were common by the early 1800s.

Both hard cider and applejack fared well until the 1830s. By 1833, there were more than six thousand organizations in the United States devoted to encouraging, in moderation, alcohol consumption, as well as abstinence. Consumers began drinking nonalcoholic, carbonated beverages, and radicals were determined to chop down apple trees in an effort to prevent the production of alcoholic apple beverages altogether.

By the turn of the nineteenth century, soft cider had replaced the hard version throughout the colonies, and the apple business turned its eye to the fresh market. No doubt there remained somewhat of a black market for applejack and such. Today, hard cider–also known as "Jersey lightning"–enjoys limited popularity, and a handful of producers are attempting to create a larger market for the product in Pennsylvania, as well as throughout the United States.

Cider is produced in large scale by companies like Zeiglers, located in Lansdale, Pennsylvania, and in smaller quantities on the orchards themselves. Small producers dot the Pennsylvania countryside, and although they use less elaborate methods to make their cider, the results are just as flavorful.

To ensure a safe product, many makers pasteurize their cider. However, consumers loyal to raw cider insist that it tastes better and seek it out at roadside stands and markets when apple season is at its peak.

Initially, apple cider is not too different from apple juice, but additional processing filters and clarifies the liquid sold as juice. As a result, apple cider contains more pectin and solids.

To make cider, apples are broken and mashed into small pieces, then pressed. Large producers generally use rack and cloth presses. The apples are washed and inspected, then fed through a grinding mill to create a pulp that looks similar to applesauce, but with skin and seeds included. The skins contribute flavor and aroma to the cider.

The pulp is then pumped or scooped into strong, woven cheesecloth placed in a wooden frame. The frame is suspended on a rack of oak slats. Several cloths are filled with the pulp and stacked in the multiple frames and racks. The pulp is pressed under two to three thousand pounds of pressure per square inch, resulting in cider that seeps out through the cheesecloth and into tubs below. The residue that is left behind, known as pomace, is often used for compost or animal feed. The cider is filtered again, pasteurized, and pumped into refrigerated tanks for storage. A thousand pounds of apples will yield about fifty gallons of cider, on average.

Nutritional Value

Although most of the colonists enjoyed apples primarily for their flavor and texture, some grew to appreciate the fruit for its nutritional value, too. Apples were sought for medicinal applications such as anesthetics, antiseptics, stimulants, and sedatives. Yet consumers knew little about the nutritional benefits beyond the basics. Today we know that one medium apple provides 160 milligrams of potassium, up to 5 grams of fiber, and 8 milligrams of vitamin C and has about 80 calories.

Contemporary research offers many reasons to consume at least one apple a day. Researchers at the Mayo Clinic report that quercetin, a plant-based nutrient found most abundantly in apples, may provide a new method for preventing or treating prostate cancer, and a study

1960s promotional ad boasts the quality of Pennsylvania and other eastern states' apples.

showed a relationship between the consumption of quercetin and a reduced risk of lung cancer. Another study showed that a modest diet of apples could improve lung function. In vitro studies at Cornell University revealed that phytonutrients in apples may inhibit the growth of colon and liver cancer cells. Researchers at the University of California–Davis have reported that daily consumption of apples and apple juice may help reduce damage caused by cholesterol and help protect against heart disease. Cornell researchers also claim that just two-thirds of an unpeeled fresh apple provide the same total antioxidant activity as fifteen hundred milligrams of vitamin C.

Apple

APPLE VARIETY USAGE

Variety	Fresh	Salads	Pies	Sauce	Baked
Braeburn	X	X	X	X	X
Cortland	X	X	X	X	X
Empire	X	X		X	
Fuji	X	X	X	X	X
Gala	X	X			
Ginger Gold	X	X	X	X	X
Golden Delicious	X	X	X	X	X
Granny Smith	X	X	X	X	X
Jonagold	X		X		X
Jonathan	X			X	
McIntosh	X			X	
Mutsu, or Crispin	X		X		X
Nittany	X	X	X	X	X
Red Delicious	X	X			
Rome			X	X	X
Stayman/Winesap	X	X	X	X	X
York Imperial	X	X	X	X	X

Recipes

Choose apples that are firm and bruise-free. Apples that are too ripe will feel soft to the touch, and the texture will be mushy and mealy. Apples that are not fully mature will be hard, with a sour, underdeveloped flavor. Although fine for cooking, underripe apples should be refrigerated for a week or two to develop their flavor before eating out of hand.

Select apple varieties based on planned use, as some varieties work best for baking, others for canning, and still others for salads. Refer to the Apple Variety Usage chart on page 56 for guidelines on which ones to use in various cooking and baking applications.

Commercial growers store their apples in controlled atmosphere (CA) storage, which reduces the apples' oxygen intake, thereby keeping them crisp and fresh for weeks, even months. At home, poke holes in a plastic bag and place your apples in it. Store in the fruit and vegetable hydrator drawer of the refrigerator at thirty-two to forty degrees fahrenheit. Pick through the apples occasionally, removing any that have spoiled. (The old adage "One bad apple will spoil the bunch" is true.) Although apples look pretty in a country crock on the kitchen table, they will not stay crisp and fresh for long.

Early-season apples, often called summer apples, generally do not keep as well as late-season varieties and may stay fresh for just a few days, even when refrigerated. Ginger Gold and Paula Red are examples of summer apple varieties that need to be kept cool and consumed quickly after purchase for optimum enjoyment.

APPLE MATH

3 medium apples equal about 1 pound

1 medium apple equals about 1 cup chopped apple

1 bushel of apples equals 42 pounds

1 cup apple juice or sauce equals about 8 ounces

Pork Chops with Creamy Apple Sauce

2 tablespoons olive oil, divided
4 lean, boneless pork chops, 1 inch thick
2 cloves garlic, crushed
salt and pepper
3 apples, peeled, cored, and sliced
1 tablespoon golden brown sugar
1 teaspoon ground mace
dash cloves and ginger
1/2 cup light cream
1/4 cup apple juice or cider

In large skillet, heat 1 tablespoon olive oil over medium heat. Add pork chops and garlic. Season with salt and pepper to taste. Brown 2 minutes per side. Transfer to paper towel–lined plate. Discard any fat from skillet. Add remaining 1 tablespoon olive oil and heat over medium heat. Add apple slices. Sprinkle with brown sugar and spices. Sauté 4 minutes or until golden. Whisk in cream and apple juice or cider. Stir constantly until cream is bubbly. Return pork chops to cream mixture. Reduce heat to low. Cover skillet and simmer 20 minutes, or until pork is tender and tests done. Serve hot. *Makes 4 servings.*

Country Ribs with Apples

2 pounds country-style beef or pork ribs, fat trimmed
1 bay leaf
salt and pepper
4 apples, peeled, cored, and chopped
2 tablespoons honey
1 teaspoon cider vinegar
2 cloves garlic, crushed
2 tablespoons ketchup

Place ribs in large saucepan and cover with cold water. Add bay leaf. Cover pan and bring to boil. Reduce heat and simmer 30 minutes. Remove from heat. Drain ribs and transfer to rack over roasting pan. Salt and pepper to taste. Set aside. Combine remaining ingredients in medium saucepan. Cover and bring to boil over medium heat. Reduce heat and simmer, stirring occasionally, until apples are very tender and mixture is smooth. Spoon and brush some of the apple mixture over ribs. Roast at 350 degrees for 45 minutes, or until meat tests done, occasionally turning and brushing with additional apple mixture while roasting. Serve hot. *Makes 2 to 4 servings.*

Applesauce Meatloaf

2 pounds lean ground beef
1 cup fine cracker crumbs
1 cup applesauce
2 eggs, slightly beaten
1/4 cup finely chopped onion
1/4 cup catsup
1 teaspoon salt
1/4 teaspoon pepper
1 tablespoon Worcestershire sauce

In large bowl, combine all ingredients except Worcestershire sauce, mixing well. Shape into loaf and place on lightly oiled rack over broiler pan. Brush top with Worcestershire sauce. Bake, uncovered, at 350 degrees for 1 hour and 15 minutes, or until done. Internal temperature should be 160 degrees. Slice and serve warm. *Makes 8 servings.*

Schnitz un Knepp

4 cups dried apple slices
3 pounds lean cooked ham
2 tablespoons packed light brown sugar
2 cups all-purpose flour
4 teaspoons baking powder
1 teaspoon salt
1/4 teaspoon pepper
1 egg, beaten
3 tablespoons butter, melted
few teaspoons milk

Place dried apple slices (schnitz) in large bowl. Cover with water. Cover and refrigerate several hours or overnight. In large cook pot, place rehydrated apples with the water used for soaking them. Add ham. Cover and simmer over medium heat 30 to 45 minutes. Add brown sugar. Remove from heat and set aside. In separate bowl, combine flour, baking powder, salt, and pepper. Add egg and melted butter. Gradually add milk, one teaspoonful at a time, until moist but stiff dough forms. Remove ham from cooking liquid and set aside, keeping warm. Bring cooking liquid to a boil. Drop dough by rounded teaspoonfuls into boiling liquid, stirring often to prevent sticking. Reduce heat; cover and simmer 15 to 20 minutes, stirring occasionally, until dumplings (knepp) are cooked through. Serve hot schnitz and knepp with slices of ham. *Makes 8 to 10 servings.*

Seashore Stir-Fry

1/4 cup butter
1 sweet onion, cut into 8 wedges
2 stalks celery, sliced
1 pound scallops
2 apples, peeled, cored, and coarsely chopped
2 tablespoons dry white wine or apple juice
salt and pepper
lemon wedges

Melt butter in large, heavy skillet or wok. Add onion and celery. Stir-fry about 3 minutes. Add scallops, apples, and wine or apple juice. Stir-fry just until scallops are cooked through. Salt and pepper to taste. Serve with lemon wedges. *Makes 4 servings.*

Apple-Beef Stew

1 pound lean beef, cubed
1 tablespoon vegetable oil
3 cups apple juice
1 teaspoon salt
1/4 teaspoon pepper
1/4 teaspoon caraway seeds
1 bay leaf
8 small carrots
4 small onions
2 apples, peeled, cored, and chopped
2 tablespoons all-purpose flour
2 tablespoons cold water

In large, heavy skillet, brown beef in oil. Stir in apple juice, salt, pepper, caraway seeds, and bay leaf. Cover and simmer 45 minutes, stirring occasionally. Add carrots and onions. Cover and continue cooking an additional 30 minutes. Stir in apples and cook 5 more minutes. Remove and discard bay leaf. In small bowl, thoroughly combine flour and cold water. Whisk into meat mixture, stirring constantly, until thickened and bubbly. Serve hot. *Makes 4 servings.*

Apple Frittata

1 tablespoon vegetable oil
1 medium onion, chopped
1 green bell pepper, chopped
1 clove garlic, crushed
1 medium apple, peeled, cored, and sliced
4 eggs
2 tablespoons water
salt and pepper to taste
1/3 cup shredded cheddar cheese

Heat oil in medium skillet. Add onion, bell pepper, and garlic. Cook over medium-low heat, stirring occasionally, until tender. Add sliced apple and cook about 4 minutes, or until tender. In medium bowl, beat eggs with water, salt, and pepper. Pour over apple-vegetable mixture in skillet. Sprinkle with cheese. Cover skillet and cook over low heat about 10 minutes, or until eggs are set and cheese melts. *Makes 2 servings.*

Glazed Apples and Carrots

10 fresh carrots, scrubbed or peeled, and sliced
5 apples, peeled, cored, and sliced
1 teaspoon fresh lemon juice
6 tablespoons golden brown sugar
3 tablespoons butter
dash salt

Place carrot slices in steamer basket. Toss apple slices with lemon juice, and add to carrots in steamer. Cover and steam just until tender. Meanwhile, in large saucepan, combine brown sugar, butter, and salt. Stir constantly over medium heat until butter is melted and sugar dissolves. Add steamed carrots and apples, turning to coat with glaze. Serve hot. *Makes 8 servings.*

Baked Acorn Squash and Apples

3 acorn squash
3 apples, cored and diced (do not peel)
3/4 cup walnuts or pecans
1/4 cup butter, melted
1/2 cup maple syrup

Cut squash in halves and remove seeds. Arrange in baking pan, cut sides up. Set aside. Toss apples with nuts. Spoon into squash. Drizzle with melted butter and maple syrup. Pour hot water around squash in baking pan to 1/2-inch depth. Cover loosely with foil. Bake at 400 degrees for 45 minutes, or until squash is tender. *Makes 6 servings.*

Fried Apples

1/4 cup butter
1/3 cup packed light brown sugar
4 apples, cored and cut into rings (do not peel)

Melt butter in large skillet. Stir in brown sugar. Add apple rings. Cook slowly, turning occasionally, until tender but still holding shape. Serve hot. *Makes 4 servings.*

Mulligatawny Soup

2 tablespoons olive oil
1 medium carrot, chopped
1 medium onion, chopped
1 stalk celery, sliced
2 apples, peeled, cored, and diced
2 tablespoons all-purpose flour
1 tablespoon curry powder
5 cups chicken broth
1 cup cooked rice
1/2 cup light cream

Heat oil in large saucepan. Add carrot, onion, and celery. Sauté 5 minutes. Add apples. Sauté 5 more minutes. Stir in flour and curry powder. Gradually whisk in chicken broth. Bring to boil. Reduce heat and cover. Simmer 20 minutes. Add rice and simmer additional 10 minutes. Remove from heat. In small saucepan, heat cream just until small bubbles form around edge of pan. Stir into soup. Serve hot. *Makes 6 servings.*

Tortellini Apple Salad

Tortellini Apple Salad

DRESSING

3 tablespoons frozen, thawed apple juice concentrate
3 tablespoons honey
1 to 2 teaspoons apple cider vinegar

Combine all dressing ingredients. Whisk to blend well. Set aside.

(continued on facing page)

SALAD

1 9-ounce package refrigerated cheese-filled tortellini
3 apples, cored and chopped (do not peel)
2 cups ready-to-serve salad greens
1 cup mandarin orange segments, drained well
1/2 cup chopped green onion
2 tablespoons chopped walnuts

Cook tortellini according to package directions. (Do not overcook.) Rinse under cold water until cooled, and drain thoroughly. In large bowl, toss tortellini with apples, salad greens, mandarin oranges, green onion, walnuts, and dressing. Serve immediately. *Makes about 8 servings.*

Fresh Apple Salad with Yogurt Dressing

1 medium apple, cored and chopped
1 banana, sliced
1 avocado, sliced
1/4 cup pineapple chunks, drained (reserve juice)
1/4 cup chopped walnuts
1/2 cup plain yogurt
2 tablespoons reserved pineapple juice
2 teaspoons sugar
1/4 teaspoon ground nutmeg

In large bowl, combine apple, banana, avocado, pineapple, and walnuts. In small bowl, combine yogurt, pineapple juice, sugar, and nutmeg. Drizzle over apple mixture and toss to coat. Serve at room temperature or refrigerate until ready to serve. *Makes 6 servings.*

Classic Waldorf Salad

4 apples, cored and chopped (do not peel)
1 cup chopped celery
1 cup walnuts
1 cup raisins
1/2 cup light mayonnaise
1 tablespoon milk
1 teaspoon sugar
salt

In large bowl, combine apples, celery, walnuts, and raisins. In small bowl, combine mayonnaise, milk, and sugar. Add to apple mixture and toss. Salt to taste. Cover and refrigerate until ready to serve. *Makes 6 servings.*

Apple Slaw

4 cups shredded red or green cabbage
3 apples, cored and chopped (do not peel)
2 medium carrots, grated
1 medium red onion, grated
2/3 cup light mayonnaise
2/3 cup light sour cream
salt and pepper

In large bowl, toss cabbage, apples, carrots, and onion. In separate bowl, combine mayonnaise and sour cream. Toss with cabbage-apple mixture. Salt and pepper to taste. Cover and refrigerate until ready to serve. *Makes 6 servings.*

Apple and Cornbread Stuffing

1/4 cup butter
1 medium onion, chopped
2 stalks celery, chopped
1/4 cup snipped fresh parsley
1 teaspoon dried oregano
2 apples, peeled, cored, and chopped
2 cups cornbread crumbs
2 tablespoons apple juice or cider
1 egg

Melt butter in large skillet. Add onion and celery. Sauté 5 minutes. Stir in parsley and oregano. Add apples and sauté 5 more minutes. Stir in cornbread crumbs. Whisk together apple juice or cider and egg. Mix into cornbread mixture. Spoon into lightly greased 1-quart baking dish. Bake at 350 degrees for 45 minutes. *Makes 6 servings.*

Apple Brown Bread

1/4 cup butter
1/3 cup molasses
1/3 cup honey
1 cup rye flour
1 cup whole wheat flour
1 cup cornmeal
2 teaspoons baking soda
1 teaspoon salt
2 cups low-fat buttermilk
2 medium apples, peeled, cored, and chopped

(continued on facing page)

Apple Brown Bread

In large bowl, beat butter with electric mixer until softened. Add molasses and honey, beating well. In separate bowl, combine rye flour, wheat flour, cornmeal, baking soda, and salt. Add about one-third to butter mixture, blending on low speed. Add half of buttermilk, beating just until blended. Add another third of flour mixture, then buttermilk, then remaining flour mixture, blending after each addition. Stir in apples. Spoon into two lightly greased 9-by-5-inch loaf pans. Bake at 325 degrees for 1 hour, or until bread tests done when toothpick inserted in center comes out clean. Cool in pans 10 minutes before removing. Serve warm or cooled. *Makes 2 loaves.*

Muffin Variation: Spoon batter into lightly greased muffin tins, custard cups, or ramekins. Bake 20 to 25 minutes, or until toothpick inserted in center comes out clean.

Apple Pancakes

- 2 cups traditional pancake mix
- 1 teaspoon sugar
- 1/4 teaspoon cinnamon
- 2 apples, peeled, cored, and finely chopped
- 1 cup milk
- 1 egg
- 1 tablespoon vegetable oil

In large bowl, combine pancake mix, sugar, and cinnamon. Stir in apples. Add milk, egg and oil. Pour by quarter cupfuls onto hot, lightly greased griddle, turning once. *Makes about 12 servings.*

Harvest Coffeecake

- 1/3 cup butter
- 1 cup sugar
- 2 eggs
- 1 teaspoon vanilla extract
- 1 1/2 cups all-purpose flour
- 2 teaspoons baking powder
- 1/2 teaspoon ground nutmeg
- 1/4 teaspoon salt
- 2/3 cup milk
- 4 apples, peeled, cored, and finely chopped
- 1 tablespoon ground cinnamon
- 1 tablespoon sugar
- 1/2 cup chopped walnuts

In large bowl, beat together butter and sugar with mixer until fluffy. Blend in eggs and vanilla extract. In separate bowl, combine flour, baking powder, nutmeg, and salt. Blend into butter mixture along with milk. Stir in apples. Pour into 9-inch square pan lightly coated with vegetable oil cooking spray. Combine cinnamon, sugar, and walnuts. Sprinkle evenly over batter in pan. Bake at 375 degrees for 25 to 30 minutes, or until cake tests done. *Makes 8 to 10 servings.*

Harvest Coffeecake

Fresh Apple Muffins

3/4 cup milk
1 egg, slightly beaten
1/4 cup butter, melted
2 cups all-purpose flour
1/2 cup sugar
1 tablespoon baking powder
1/2 teaspoon salt
1/2 teaspoon ground cinnamon
1 apple, peeled, cored, and finely chopped
1/2 cup raisins

In small bowl, combine milk and egg. Stir in melted butter. Set aside. In large bowl, combine flour, sugar, baking powder, salt, and cinnamon. Stir in apples and raisins. Stir in milk-egg mixture just until dry ingredients are moistened. Fill lightly greased muffin tins three-quarters full with batter. Bake at 400 degrees for 20 to 25 minutes, or until golden brown. *Makes 10 to 12 muffins.*

Harvest Apple Cake

CAKE

2 cups sugar
3/4 cup vegetable oil
2 eggs
1 tablespoon vanilla extract
2 cups all-purpose flour
2 teaspoons ground cinnamon
1 1/2 teaspoons baking soda
1/2 teaspoon salt
4 cups cored, peeled, and chopped apples
1 cup chopped walnuts
1 cup raisins

In large bowl, beat together sugar and oil with mixer. Blend in eggs and vanilla extract. In separate bowl, combine flour, cinnamon, baking soda, and salt. Blend into sugar-oil mixture. Stir in apples, walnuts, and raisins. Pour into lightly greased and floured 13-by-9-inch baking pan. Bake at 350 degrees for 40 to 45 minutes, or until cake is set in center. Cool completely.

FROSTING

8-ounce package cream cheese
1/2 cup softened butter
2 teaspoons vanilla extract
1-pound box confectioners' sugar

In large bowl, beat cream cheese until softened. Blend in softened butter and vanilla extract. Gradually add confectioners' sugar, blending until smooth and creamy. Frost cooled cake. *Makes 8 to 10 servings.*

Apple Crisp

6 cups peeled and sliced apples
3/4 cup all-purpose flour
3/4 cup packed brown sugar
1/2 teaspoon cinnamon
dash salt
1/2 cup cold butter
whipped topping or vanilla ice cream

Place apple slices in lightly greased, medium baking dish. In medium bowl, combine flour, brown sugar, cinnamon, and salt. Cut in butter with fork or pastry cutter until crumbly. Sprinkle over apples in dish. Bake at 350 degrees for 35 to 40 minutes, or until apples are tender. Serve warm with whipped topping or ice cream. *Makes 6 servings.*

Apple Pandowdy

FILLING

4 apples, peeled, cored, and sliced
1/4 cup sugar
1/2 teaspoon cinnamon
2 tablespoons butter

Arrange apple slices in lightly greased 9-inch square pan. Combine sugar and cinnamon and sprinkle over apples. Dot with butter. Set aside while preparing topping.

TOPPING

1/2 cup butter
1/2 cup sugar
1 egg, slightly beaten
1 teaspoon vanilla extract
1/2 cup all-purpose flour
1/2 teaspoon baking powder
1/4 teaspoon salt
vanilla ice cream

In large bowl, beat butter to soften. Add sugar and beat until creamy. Blend in egg and vanilla extract. In separate bowl, combine flour, baking powder, and salt. Stir into butter mixture until blended well. Drop by generous spoonfuls onto apples in pan. Bake at 350 degrees for 30 to 35 minutes, or until lightly browned. Serve warm with vanilla ice cream. *Makes 8 servings.*

Classic Apple Pie

Apple Crumb Pie

4 large apples, cored, peeled, and sliced
1 cup sugar, divided
1 teaspoon cinnamon
1/8 teaspoon salt
9-inch unbaked pie crust
3/4 cup all-purpose flour
1/3 cup butter

Line 9-inch pie plate with crust. Toss apple slices with 1/2 cup of the sugar, cinnamon, and salt. Spoon into unbaked pie crust. In bowl, combine remaining 1/2 cup sugar and flour. Cut up butter and add to sugar-flour mixture, mixing with fork until coarse crumbs form. Sprinkle over apples in crust. Bake at 425 degrees for 10 minutes. Reduce temperature to 350 degrees, and bake 40 more minutes. Serve slightly warm or cool. *Makes 6 to 8 servings.*

Classic Apple Pie

> "If you truly wish to make an apple pie from scratch, you must first create the universe."—Carl Sagan

two 9-inch unbaked pie crusts
3/4 cup sugar
2 tablespoons all-purpose flour
1 teaspoon ground cinnamon
1/8 teaspoon ground nutmeg
1/8 teaspoon salt
5 large apples, cored, peeled, and sliced
2 tablespoons butter

Line 9-inch pie plate with one pie crust. Set aside. In large bowl, combine sugar, flour, cinnamon, nutmeg, and salt. Add apple slices, tossing well. Spoon into pastry-lined pie plate. Cut butter into small pieces and arrange over top. Place second pie crust over top. Seal edges and slit top to allow steam to escape. Bake at 400 degrees for 15 minutes. Reduce temperature to 350 degrees and bake 25 to 30 more minutes. *Makes 6 to 8 servings.*

Sour Cream Apple Pie

PIE

1 cup sour cream
2 eggs
1/2 cup sugar
2 tablespoons all-purpose flour
1 teaspoon vanilla extract
4 medium apples, cored, peeled, and thinly sliced
9-inch unbaked pie shell

In large bowl, combine sour cream, eggs, sugar, flour, and vanilla extract, blending well with spoon. Fold in apple slices. Spoon into unbaked pie shell. Set aside.

TOPPING

1/4 cup packed light or golden brown sugar
2 tablespoons butter
1 tablespoon all-purpose flour
1/2 teaspoon cinnamon
1/4 cup chopped walnuts

In small bowl, combine brown sugar, butter, flour, and cinnamon. Stir in walnuts. Sprinkle mixture evenly over top of pie. Bake at 400 degrees for 15 minutes. Reduce oven to 300 degrees and bake 45 more minutes, or until crust is lightly browned. Serve slightly warm or at room temperature with sweetened whipped cream. *Makes 8 servings.*

Pennsylvania Apple Dumplings

SYRUP

- 1/3 cup all-purpose flour
- 1 1/2 cups sugar
- 1/4 teaspoon ground cinnamon
- 1/4 teaspoon salt
- 1 1/2 cups water
- 1 1/2 tablespoons butter

In small saucepan, combine all syrup ingredients except butter. Bring to boil over medium heat, stirring constantly. Add butter and stir until melted and blended. Remove from heat and set aside while preparing pastry and dumplings.

PASTRY

- 2 cups all-purpose flour
- 1/2 teaspoon salt
- 3/4 cup vegetable shortening (do not use oil, butter, or margarine)
- 1/2 cup cold water

In large bowl, combine flour and salt. Cut in shortening with pastry blender or knife until coarse crumbs form. Stir in cold water just until flour mixture is moistened and clings together. Using well-floured rolling pin, roll out dough to 18-by-12-inch rectangle on generously floured surface. Cut dough into six 6-inch squares.

DUMPLINGS

- 6 medium apples, peeled and cored
- 1 cup sugar
- 1 teaspoon cinnamon
- vanilla ice cream

Place an apple on each pastry square. In small bowl, combine sugar and cinnamon. Sprinkle into centers of apples. Fold dough up and around apples, bringing four corners together on top. Pinch edges together to seal shut. Arrange apples in ungreased 13-by-9-inch oblong baking pan. Bake at 375 degrees for 40 to 45 minutes, or until golden brown. Serve warm with vanilla ice cream. *Makes 6 servings.*

Baked Apples

4 apples
1/4 cup sugar
4 teaspoons light brown sugar
1 tablespoon butter
1/4 teaspoon cinnamon
1/8 teaspoon nutmeg
1/2 cup water

Core apples part of the way through (do not peel). Arrange in baking dish. In center of each, place 1 tablespoon sugar and 1 teaspoon brown sugar. Top with butter. Sprinkle with cinnamon and nutmeg. Pour 1/2 cup water around apples in dish. Bake at 350 degrees for 35 to 40 minutes, or until apples are tender but still hold shape. Serve hot. *Makes 4 servings.*

Applesauce Bread Pudding

16 thin slices cinnamon-raisin bread
1/2 cup butter, softened
2 cups applesauce
1 cup packed light or golden brown sugar
1 tablespoon ground cinnamon
1/2 teaspoon ground nutmeg
8 large eggs
6 cups whole milk
1 teaspoon vanilla extract
sweetened whipped cream

Spread one side of each bread slice with softened butter. Lightly coat 3-quart glass baking dish with vegetable oil cooking spray. Arrange half of the bread slices in baking dish, buttered side up, trimming bread to cover bottom of dish completely. Spoon and spread applesauce on top. Set aside. In small bowl, combine brown sugar, cinnamon, and nutmeg. Sprinkle evenly over applesauce in dish. Layer remaining bread slices on top, buttered side down. In large bowl, whisk or beat together eggs, milk, and vanilla extract. Pour over bread mixture in baking dish. Bake at 350 degrees for 45 to 60 minutes, or until puffy and browned. Serve warm with sweetened whipped cream. *Makes 10 servings.*

Apple and Cheese Crescents

2 packages (8-ounce) refrigerated crescent dinner rolls
4 slices American cheese
3 apples, peeled, cored, and thinly sliced
3 tablespoons sugar
1 teaspoon ground cinnamon

Separate crescent roll dough as directed on package, and arrange on large, ungreased baking sheet. Cut each slice of cheese into four triangles. Lay triangle of cheese on each crescent, near bottom. Arrange apple slices on top. In small bowl, combine sugar and cinnamon. Sprinkle over apple slices. Roll up crescents. Bake at 350 degrees for 15 to 20 minutes, or until golden brown. *Makes 16 servings.*

Apple Fritters

1 egg
3/4 cup milk
1/2 teaspoon vanilla extract
1 cup all-purpose flour
2 tablespoons sugar
2 teaspoons baking powder
1/4 teaspoon salt
4 apples, peeled, cored, and sliced into rings
vegetable oil
confectioners' sugar

In large bowl, beat egg, milk, and vanilla extract with wire whisk or fork until blended well. Stir in flour, sugar, baking powder, and salt. Dip apple rings in flour mixture, turning to coat completely. In large, heavy skillet, heat 1/4-inch depth of vegetable oil to 365 degrees. Place apple rings in hot oil. Fry until golden brown, turning once. Transfer to paper towels to drain. Roll in confectioners' sugar. Serve hot. *Makes about 16 servings.*

Johnny Appleseed Cookies

COOKIES

1/2 cup butter
1 cup packed light brown sugar
1 egg
1/4 cup milk
2 1/4 cups all-purpose flour
1 teaspoon baking powder
1 teaspoon baking soda
1/2 teaspoon salt
1/4 teaspoon cinnamon
1/4 teaspoon nutmeg
2 cups peeled and grated apples
1/2 cup chopped walnuts or pecans

In large mixing bowl, beat butter until softened. Add brown sugar and beat until creamy. Add egg and milk, blending well. In separate bowl, combine flour, baking powder, baking soda, salt, cinnamon, and nutmeg. Stir into butter mixture with apples and nuts, blending well. Drop by rounded teaspoonfuls onto lightly greased cookie sheets. Bake at 375 degrees for 10 to 12 minutes. Meanwhile, make glaze.

VANILLA GLAZE

1 cup confectioners' sugar
1 tablespoon softened butter
1 tablespoon milk
1/2 teaspoon vanilla extract

In medium bowl, combine sugar, butter, milk, and vanilla. Beat until smooth and creamy. If too thick, add small amount of additional milk. Top cookies with glaze while still warm. Cool completely. *Makes about 3 dozen.*

Apple and Date Squares

1/2 cup butter
3/4 cup sugar
1 egg
1 1/2 cups all-purpose flour
1 teaspoon baking soda
1/4 teaspoon salt
2 apples, peeled, cored, and finely chopped
1 cup chopped dates
1/4 cup golden brown sugar
1 teaspoon ground cinnamon
1/2 cup chopped walnuts
vanilla ice cream or whipped topping

In large bowl, beat together butter and sugar with mixer until fluffy. Blend in egg. In separate bowl, combine flour, baking soda, and salt. Blend into butter-sugar mixture just until smooth. Stir in apples and dates. Spread into 9-inch square baking pan lightly coated with vegetable oil cooking spray. In small bowl, toss together brown sugar, cinnamon, and walnuts. Sprinkle evenly over batter in pan. Bake at 350 degrees for 30 to 35 minutes, or until set. Cut into squares and serve slightly warm with ice cream or whipped topping. *Makes 8 to 10 servings.*

Caramel Apples

6 apples
6 wooden sticks or skewers
14-ounce package caramels
3 tablespoons water
finely chopped nuts

Wash and dry apples with clean paper towels. Insert wooden sticks or skewers in stem ends. Set aside. Place caramels and water in medium saucepan over low heat. Stir constantly until melted and smooth. Dip apples in melted caramel, turning to coat completely. Roll in chopped nuts. Transfer to waxed-paper-lined tray. Let stand until caramel coating is set.

Hot Spiced Cider

Hot Spiced Cider

4 cups apple cider
1 cup orange juice
1/2 cup fresh lemon juice
2 tablespoons honey
1 stick cinnamon
3 whole cloves
1/8 teaspoon ground allspice
1 teaspoon butter

Combine all ingredients except butter in medium saucepan. Bring to simmer over medium heat. Reduce heat and cover. Simmer 30 minutes. Remove cinnamon stick and cloves. Add butter, stirring and heating just until melted. Serve hot. *Makes 8 servings.*

Hot Apple Punch

4 cups apple juice or cider
2 cups cranberry juice
1 cup orange juice
1/2 cup freshly squeezed lemon juice
3/4 cup sugar
3 whole cloves
1 teaspoon ground allspice
2 cinnamon sticks

Combine all ingredients in large kettle. Cover and bring to boil, stirring occasionally. Reduce heat. Remove and discard cloves and cinnamon sticks. Serve hot. *Makes 10 to 12 servings.*

Apple Tea

6 cups apple juice
1 tablespoon honey
4 whole cloves
1 stick cinnamon, broken
2 tea bags

Combine all ingredients except tea bags in large saucepan. Cover and bring to boil. Turn off heat. Add tea bags, cover, and steep 3 to 5 minutes. Remove and discard tea bags, cloves, and cinnamon. Serve hot. *Makes 6 servings.*

Brandied Apple Butter

6 apples, peeled, cored, and quartered
1 orange, peeled and sliced
1½ cups water
1 cup sugar
½ teaspoon cinnamon
¼ teaspoon cloves
¼ teaspoon allspice
½ cup peach brandy

Place fruits and water in large saucepan. Cover and cook over medium heat, stirring occasionally, until fruit is very tender. Press through sieve or food mill, discarding skin and seeds. Return cooked apple pulp to saucepan. Add sugar and spices. Cook over medium heat, stirring occasionally, until mixture is thickened. Add brandy. Spoon into clean jars and seal with clean lids. Refrigerate until ready to serve. Makes an excellent hostess gift. *Makes about 2 cups.*

Cran-Apple Chutney

2 cups apples, cored, peeled, and chopped
1 cup fresh cranberries
¼ cup golden raisins
2 tablespoons golden brown sugar
2 tablespoons cider vinegar
1 tablespoon fresh orange zest
¼ teaspoon ground cloves
¼ teaspoon ground nutmeg
¼ teaspoon ground cinnamon

Combine all ingredients in medium saucepan. Bring to boil over medium-high heat, stirring constantly. Reduce heat and simmer, uncovered, for 15 minutes. Remove from heat and cool slightly. Transfer to blender or food processor. Cover and process a few seconds until smooth. Serve warm over waffles, pound cake, or ice cream. *Makes 4 servings.*

Minted Apple Vinegar

1 cup fresh apple mint leaves
2 cups apple cider vinegar

Gently rinse apple mint leaves in cold water. Drain and lay on paper towels. Cover with additional paper towels. Air-dry 2 to 3 hours. Combine mint leaves with vinegar in glass bowl. Cover tightly and let stand at room temperature for 3 to 4 weeks. Stir occasionally. Strain vinegar through cheesecloth or coffee filter and discard leaves. Pour vinegar into decorative bottle and add one fresh apple mint leaf. Seal with a cork. Wrap raffia or ribbon around the neck of the bottle and tie, making a bow. Makes a wonderful hostess gift. Excellent as a lamb or pork marinade or combined with oil for salad dressing.

Guide to Pennsylvania Apple Festivals and Farm Markets

The freshest apples are those plucked right from the tree, and Pennsylvania offers many "pick-your-own" orchards and farm markets, as well as festivals featuring the delicious fruit. Take a drive through Pennsylvania's apple country during the late summer and fall to find plenty of places to pick apples or purchase them from a market or stand, or check out one of the festivals listed below for family-oriented fun.

Pennsylvania Apple Festivals

Apple Blossom Festival

South Mountain Fairgrounds
Arendtsville, PA
717-677-7444

Modest admission fee
Held the first Saturday and Sunday in May, from 9 A.M. to 5 P.M.
An old-fashioned country festival, featuring handmade crafts, orchard tours, agricultural displays, entertainment, contests, and plenty of fresh apples and prepared apple foods

National Apple Harvest Festival

South Mountain Fairgrounds
Arendtsville, PA
717-677-7444

Modest admission fee
Held the first and second Saturday and Sunday in October, from 8 A.M. to 6 P.M.

One of the country's largest apple festivals, featuring plenty of entertainment, apple products and treats, orchard tours, Johnny Appleseed pie-eating and apple-bobbing contest, antique autos, and a photography contest, among other activities (see also page 21)

New Cumberland Apple Festival

New Cumberland Town Park
New Cumberland, PA
717-774-0404
www.newcumberlandpa.com/applefes.html

Free admission
Held the last Saturday in September, from 9 A.M. to 5 P.M.
Features food, crafts, fine art, children's activities, and entertainment

Hopewell Furnace Apple Harvest

2 Mark Bird Lane
Elverson, PA
610-582-8773

Modest admission
Fall dates vary with local harvests, call for schedule
Features apple desserts, tours, crafts, and entertainment

Hickory Apple Festival

Hickory, PA
724-356-3378

Free admission
Held the first Saturday and Sunday in October
Enjoy apple desserts, crafts, and entertainment

Fall Harvest Festival

Trax Farms Market
Route 88
Finleyville, PA
412-835-3246
www.traxfarms.com

Free admission
Held every weekend in October, 10 A.M. to 5 P.M.
Features apple recipes, decorations, hayrides, and children's play area

Apple Festival

Heller Orchard
Route 239
Wapwallopen, PA
570-379-3953
www.councilcup.com/AppleFestival

Free admission
Held Saturday (10 A.M. to 5 P.M.) and Sunday (11 A.M. to 5 P.M.) in mid-October, call for specific dates
Enjoy apple baked goods and festival activities

Apple Fest on the Green

Montrose, PA
570-278-9027

Free admission
Held Saturday in mid-September, 8 A.M. to 4 P.M., call for specific date
Features apple pie–eating contests, bike races, bake sale

Seven Sweet and Sours Festival

Kitchen Kettle Village
Intercourse, PA
800-732-3538
www.kitchenkettle.com

Free admission
Held one Thursday through Saturday each September, with varying daytime hours
One of Lancaster County's largest harvest events, featuring demonstrations, recipes, food, and fun

Kerosene Lamp Tours

Amish Farm and House
Lancaster, PA
717-394-6185
www.amishfarmandhouse.com

Modest admission possible
Tours are given Saturdays from the end of September through most of October, 6 to 8 P.M.
Evening tours of an authentic Amish home, featuring apple schnitz pie and cider; hayrides

Applefest

Downtown
Franklin, PA
814-432-5823
www.franklin-pa.org/html/applefest.htm

Free parking and shuttle
Held the first Friday and Saturday in October, 10 A.M. to dusk
Features delicious apple treats, entertainment, arts and crafts, children's activities, antique car show, 5K race, and live shows

Pennsylvania Apple and Cheese Festival

Manley-Bohlayer Farm
Canton, PA
570-673-5500
www.rekindlethespirit.com

Modest admission
Held the first Saturday (10 A.M. to 6 P.M.) and Sunday (10 A.M. to 5 P.M.) in October
Features apple pie and cheesecake contests, arts and crafts, photography, an auction, and continuous, free entertainment

Annual Fall Foliage Festival

Downtown
Bedford, PA
800-765-3331
www.bedfordcounty.net/fall

Free admission
Held the first and second Saturday (9 A.M. to 5 P.M.) and Sunday (11 A.M. to 5 P.M.) in October
Features apple cider making and hourly entertainment; more than four hundred craft exhibits, antique car and wagon train parades, quilt show and sale

Pennsylvania Farm Markets

* pick-your-own apple sales.

Adams County

Apple A Day Farm Market
2915 Biglerville Road
Gettysburg, PA 17325
717-677-8051

Barbour's Fruit Farm
4045 Chambersburg Road
Biglerville, PA 17307
717-334-0178

*Beechwood Orchards
984 Carlisle Road
Biglerville, PA 17307
717-677-6536

Boyer Nurseries and Orchards
405 Boyer Nursery Road
Biglerville, PA 17307
717-677-8558
www.boyernurseries.com

Buttercup Farm Market
1246B Route 194 North
Abbottstown, PA 17301
717-259-6594

Countryside Gardens
2440 Baltimore Pike
Gettysburg, PA 17325
717-334-8321

Donaldson Farm Market
3345 Fairfield Road
Gettysburg, PA 17325
717-642-6223

Fair Field Farm
341 Fairfield Station Road
Fairfield, PA 17320
717-642-9004

Flickinger's Produce
2245 Bon-Ox Road
New Oxford, PA 17350
717-624-8036

Gray Wolf Plantation
350 Forest Drive
New Oxford, PA 17350
717-624-7204
www.graywolfplantation.com

Highfield Hollow Farm
150 Hill Top Road
Gardners, PA 17324
717-528-4825

Hollabaugh Brothers Fruit
Farm and Market
481 Carlisle Road
Biglerville, PA 17307
717-677-9494
www.hollabaughbros.com

Honda Acres Farm
and Flea Market
170 Honda Road
Littlestown, PA 17340
717-359-5429

Kuhn Orchards
1041 Old Route 30
Cashtown, PA 17310
717-334-2722

Marti's Broad Valley
Orchard Market
1934 Wenksville Road
Biglerville, PA 17307
717-677-4131

The Peters Orchards
10540 Carlisle Pike
Gardners, PA 17324
717-528-4380

Round Barn Farm Market
298 Cashtown Road
Biglerville, PA 17307
717-334-1984

Sandoe's Fruit Market
304 Carlisle Road
Biglerville, PA 17307
717-677-6931

Valley Enterprises
855-1091 Fairfield Station Road
Fairfield, PA 17328
717-642-5432

Weiser Orchards Fruit Stand
490 Town Hill Road
York Springs, PA 17372
717-528-4796

Woerner Orchards
1140 Carrolls Tract Road
Orrtanna, PA 17353
717-642-5230

Allegheny County

Beccari's Farm Market
5091 Thoms Run Road
Oakdale, PA 15071
412-221-8768

Blackberry Meadows Farm
7115 Ridge Road
Natrona Heights, PA 15065
724-226-3939

Eichner's Farm Market
285 Richard Road
Wexford, PA 15090
724-935-2131

Janoski's Farm Market
1714 Route 30
Clinton, PA 15026
724-899-3438

Kaelin Farms and Market
2546 Brandt School Road
Wexford, PA 15090
724-935-6780

Naylors Orchards
118 Crest Lane
Glenshaw, PA 15116
412-486-2647

Pure Earth Farm
825 Bank Street
Bridgeville, PA 15017
412-257-4982

Reilly's Summer Seat Farm
1120 Roosevelt Road
Pittsburgh, PA 15237
412-364-8662

Shenot Farm Market
3754 Wexford Run Road
Wexford, PA 15090
724-935-1743

Soergel Orchards
2573 Brandt, I-79, Exit 22
Wexford, PA 15090
724-935-1743

Triple "B" Farms
823 Berry Lane
Monongahela, PA 15063
724-258-3557

Wexford Farms
Warrendale Bakerstown Road
Wexford, PA 15090
724-625-1635

Armstrong County

Dan Hadden
R.D. 1
Smicksburg, PA 16256
724-286-9895

Kistaco Farm Market
3483 Balsiger Road
Apollo, PA 15613
724-478-4361

Longview Farm
R.D. 1
Worthington, PA 16262
724-297-5834

Robinson's Farm Market
R.D. 2
Kittanning, PA 16201
724-545-7125

White Oak Farms
R.D. 1
Dayton, PA 16222
814-257-8485

Beaver County

Beaver County Fruit
and Garden Center
1089 North Broad Leaf Road
Chester Township, PA 15001
724-774-4402

Ber-Nita Acres
R.D. 2, 151 Bennett Drive
Ellwood City, PA 16117
724-752-1455

Brady's Run Farm Market
Route 51
Fallston, PA 15066
724-846-1030

Fausti's Farm
1017 Porter Street
Conway, PA 15027
724-869-1027

Helbling Farms
212 Little Beaver Road
Enon Valley, PA 16120
724-336-FARM

Honeydale Farm
183 Morgan Lane
Darlington, PA 16115
724-827-2654

Kretschmann Organic Farm
R.D. 1
Rochester, PA 15074
724-452-7189

New Beginnings
1163 Route 588-1
Fombell, PA 16123
724-752-8259

Schiefelbein Farm Market
3323 Route 151
2 miles west of Route 60, Exit 9
Aliquippa, PA 15001
724-378-8807

Sturges Orchards
Route 288 between Zelienople
and Ellwood City
Fombell, PA 16123
724-752-8920

Swick's Orchard
Off Route 588, 6 miles east
of Beaver Falls
Beaver Falls, PA 15010
724-843-8865

Bedford County

Boyer Orchards
4116 Cortland Drive
New Paris, PA 15554
814-839-4715

Cuppett Brothers Farm
125 Cuppett Road
New Paris, PA 15554
814-839-4492

Davis Orchard
Route 96, 4 miles south
of Pleasantville
New Paris, PA 15554
814-276-3040

Mellott Greenhouse
Route 36, 12 miles south
of Roaring Spring
Loysburg, PA 16659
814-766-2383

Mile Level Country Market
and Greenhouses
9571 Lincoln Highway
Bedford, PA 15522
814-623-5642

Ridgetop Orchard
R.D. 1
Schellsburg, PA 15559

Sleek's Orchard
2808 Cortland Road
New Paris, PA 15554
814-733-4276/4776

Sollenberger Farm Products
566 Salemville Road
New Enterprise, PA 16664
814-766-3638

Berks County

Augora Fruit Farms
502 Augora Road
Reading, PA 19606
610-921-3870

B & J Farm
187 Fancy Hill Road
Boyertown, PA 19512
610-689-5893

Bechtel's Ponderosa
843 Balthaser Road
Lenhartsville, PA 19534
610-562-5970

Beekman Orchards, Inc.
R.D. 6, Franklin Road
Boyertown, PA 19512
610-369-1568

Blue Spruce Market
Route 1
Womelsdorf, PA 19567
610-589-4374

Burkholder's Farm
Fresh Produce
R.D. 4
Fleetwood, PA 19522
610-944-0329

Burkholder's Naturals
and Organics
460 Bowers Road
Kutztown, PA 19530
610-682-7460

Cal Degler Fruit and Vegetables
2800 River Road
Reading, PA 19605
610-921-3810

Carleybrook Gardens
R.D. 4, Hartz Road
Mohnton, PA 19540
610-856-7392

Commonwealth Farms
223 Valley Road
Bernville, PA 19506
610-488-6177

Country Junction
15620 Kutztown Road
Kutztown, PA 19530
610-683-3500

Country Market
153 Dotterer Road
Lenhartsville, PA 19534
610-756-6959

County Line Orchard
9200 Kings Highway
Kempton, PA 19529
610-756-6411

Crossroad Acres
1256 Tilden Road
Mohrsville, PA 19541
610-488-6184

Ehst Homestead Farm
Star Route
Bally, PA 19503
610-845-7069

Eugene Taylor
317 Machamer Road
Douglassville, PA 19518
610-689-9422

F. M. Brown's Sons
Furnace Street
Birdsboro, PA 19508
610-582-2741

Finch Farm
151 Limekiln Road
Reading, PA 19606
610-779-3887

Frecon Orchard Outlet
501 South Reading Avenue
Boyertown, PA 19512
610-367-6200

Glenn D. Tothero
R.D. 1
Mohnton, PA 19540
610-856-7542

Henninger Nursery
324 Woods Road
Kempton, PA 19529
610-756-6897

Hobert's Fruit Farm
13 Baldy Hill Road
Alburtis, PA 18011
610-845-2198

John's Nursery
R.D. 3
Hamburg, PA 19526
610-562-8101

Johnson's Farm
121 Midway Road
Bethel, PA 19507
717-933-8868

Leon H. Martin Produce
8th and Penn Streets
Reading, PA 19601
610-372-4986

Long and Winding Row Farm
R.D. 2
Kempton, PA 19529
610-756-3578

Map Farm
R.D. 1
Womelsdorf, PA 19567
717-866-4185

Martin's Produce Stand
R.D. 2
Fleetwood, PA 19522
610-926-5828

Meadow View Farm
371 Bowers Road
Kutztown, PA 19530
610-682-6094

Mountain Hollow Farm
289 West Texter Mission Road
Robesonia, PA 19551
610-589-2169

Ontelaunee Orchards
Route 61
Leesport, PA 19533
610-926-2288

Papa Farm
749 Bloody Spring Road
Bethel, PA 19507
610-488-0801

Perry Acres
R.D. 2
Hamburg, PA 19526
610-944-9910

Pine Top Farm
65 Bitting Road
Alburtis, PA 18011
610-845-3119

Preston Orchards
168 Preston Road
Wernersville, PA 19565
610-678-8686

Reidenhour's Produce
715 Valley Road
Hamburg, PA 19526
610-562-7667

Richard D. Hershey
1763 Ramich Road
Temple, PA 19560
610-929-4637

Richmond Produce
R.D. 2
Fleetwood, PA 19522
610-944-7764

Riedel's Garden Patch
467 Route 22
Blandon, PA 19510
610-926-3676

Shanesville Orchards
Roadside Market
120 Schoolhouse Road
Boyertown, PA 19512
610-367-8496

Shirley Brothers' Orchard
1259 Old Airport Road
Douglassville, PA 19518
610-689-5361

Skyline Drive Orchard
118 Skyline Drive
Reading, PA 19606
610-929-0888

Stoudt's Ferry Orchard
4901 Stoudt's Ferry Road
Reading, PA 19605
610-926-1175

Strause's Fruit Farm
193 Mill Hill Road
Hamburg, PA 19526
610-488-6531

Strawberry Hill Farm
218 Robin Hill Road
Lenhartsville, PA 19534
610-756-4252

Sunnyside Farm
288 Shartlesville Road
Bernville, PA 19506
610-488-1662

Tim's Garden Fresh Veggies
64 Fisher Mill Road
Boyertown, PA 19512
610-689-5037

Vista Grande Farm
R.D. 4
Fleetwood, PA 19522
610-944-0541

Weaver's Orchard Farm Market
Route 2
Morgantown, PA 19543
610-856-7300

Wilcox Farms
1134 Reading Avenue
Boyertown, PA 19512
610-367-2387

Willow Springs Farm
263 Reiff Road
Oley, PA 19547
610-987-3444

Blair County

Baker's Farm Market
1114 Route 36 South
Duncansville, PA 16635
814-695-3418

Baronner Farms
North Juniata Street
Hollidaysburg, PA 16648
814-695-4522

Blueberry Hill
1527 West Carson Valley Road
Duncansville, PA 16635
814-695-1519

Bridenbaugh Farm Market
R.D. 1
Martinsburg, PA 16662
814-793-9732

Friends Farm Market
R.D. 2
Williamsburg, PA 16693
814-793-9379

Hinish Farm Market
R.D. 1, Route 36
Roaring Spring, PA 16673
814-224-5454

Imler's Greenhouse
413 4th Street
Lakemont, PA 16602
814-944-1440

Johnson's Greenhouse
R.D. 3
Altoona, PA 16601
814-943-1471

Leidig's Farm
R.D. 4
Tyrone, PA 16686
814-632-6986

Logan Spring Farm
Box 10
Bellwood, PA 16617
814-742-8118

Long Road Farm
R.D. 1
Claysburg, PA 16625
814-239-5685

Peach Hill Orchard
1027 Curryville Road
Martinsburg, PA 16662
814-793-3927

*Perry's Orchard
MR 70 Sylvan Heights Drive
Hollidaysburg, PA 16648
814-695-9518

Roudabush's Bakery
and Produce Market
R.D. 2
Claysburg, PA 16625
814-239-2595

Spring Farm Greenhouse
R.D. 1
Martinsburg, PA 16662
814-793-3954

Sunny Mead Farm
R.D. 3
Altoona, PA 16601
814-944-7489

Wagner's Greenhouses
2036 Crawford Avenue
Altoona, PA 16602
814-946-0788

Bradford County

*Bohlayer's Orchard
R.D. 1
Troy, PA 16947
570-297-2480

Dewy Meadows-Maples
HC 34
Warren Center, PA 18851
570-395-3458

Gardiner's Farm
R.R. 2, Fallbrook Road
Troy, PA 16947
570-297-3929

Gibb's Perennial Gardens
HCR 34
Leraysville, PA 18829
570-744-2717

Harris Farm Market
and Bake Shop
R.D. 1
Milan, PA 18831
570-888-2236

Hulslander's Farm
R.D. 3
Troy, PA 16947
570-297-2517

Keystone Cider Mill
419 North Keystone Avenue
Sayre, PA 18840
570-888-9475

Ludwig's Farm and Greenhouse
R.D. 1, Grimley Road
Sayre, PA 18840
570-247-2973

Marie's Produce
R.D. 4
Towanda, PA 18848
570-265-3629

M's Roadside Market
Route 414
Monroeton, PA 18832

Slipping Down Farm
R.D. 2
Athens, PA 18810
570-888-6863

Smeck's Farm Market
R.R. 2, Route 187 North
Wysox, PA 18854

Towanda Tree Farm
R.R. 1
Towanda, PA 18848
570-265-2600

Troy Fruit Stand
Canton Street
Troy, PA 16947
570-297-2292

Urban Farm
R.D. 1, Wolcott Hollow Road
Athens, PA 18810
570-888-0516

Bucks County

Active Acres
881 Highland Road
Newtown, PA 18940
215-968-2192

Bolton Farm Market
Route 113
Silverdale, PA 18962
215-257-6047

Brumbaugh's Farm
2575 County Line Road
Telford, PA 18969
215-723-3508

Bryan's Farm
2023 Second Street Pike
Richboro, PA 18954
215-598-3206

Charlann Farms
586 Stony Hill Road
Yardley, PA 19067
215-493-1831

Deere Acres
2165 Trumbauersville Road
Quakertown, PA 18951
215-536-8859

The Farm Market
at Delaware Valley College
Route 202 and New Britain Road
Doylestown, PA 18901
215-589-2918

Grover's Greenery and Produce
541 Dark Hollow Road
Pipersville, PA 18947

Hellerick's Farm
5500 Easton Road, Route 611
Doylestown, PA 18901
215-766-8388

Hidden Hollow Farm
5980 Route 263
Lahaska, PA 18931
215-794-5650

*Homestead Orchards
328 Twinbrook Road
Perkasie, PA 18944
215-257-9286

Manoff Market Gardens
Comfort Road
Solebury, PA 18963
215-297-8220

McCardle's Holiday Farm
4316 Mechanicsville Road
Mechanicsville, PA 18934
215-794-7655

Moyer's Village Farm
183 North Main Street
Dublin, PA 18917
215-249-3616

Mt. Amos Farm
1749 Narrows Hill Road
Upper Black Eddy, PA 18972
215-982-9405

Myerov Family Farm
306 Elephant Road
Perkasie, PA 18944
215-249-3145

None Such Farm
Route 263
Buckingham, PA 18912
215-794-5201

Penn Vermont Fruit Farm
Box 346
Bedminster, PA 18910
215-795-0230/2475

Penn View Farm
1433 Broad Street
Perkasie, PA 18944
215-249-3395

The Salad Garden Farm Market
527 Center Hill Road
Upper Black Eddy, PA 18972
610-847-2853

Shady Brook Farm
931 Stony Hill Road
Yardley, PA 19067
215-968-1670

*Snipes Farm and Nursery
890 West Bridge Street
Morrisville, PA 19067
215-295-7236

*Solebury Orchards
3325 Creamery Road
New Hope, PA 18938
215-297-8079

Solly Brothers
707 Almshouse Road
Ivyland, PA 18974
215-357-7660

Stovers Farm Market
5008 Anderson Road
Buckingham, PA 18912
215-794-7381

Styer Orchards
1121 Woodbourne Road
Langhorne, PA 19047
215-757-7646

Tabora Farm and Orchard
1104 Upper Stump Road
Chalfont, PA 18914
215-249-3016

*Thorpe Farm
371 Stoney Brook Road
Newtown, PA 18940
215-493-4900 or 862-2650

Trauger's Farm Market
Route 611
Kintnersville, PA 18930
610-847-5702

Wild Blue Wonder Farm Field
1024 Kellers Church Road
Bedminster, PA 18910
215-795-2409

Wildemore Farm
977 Upper Stump Road
Chalfont, PA 18914
215-249-3683

Butler County

Cool Springs Organics
830 Brownsdale Road
Evans City, PA 16033
724-538-9782

Crighton's Farm Market and Greenhouse
130 Main Street, Route 488
Prospect, PA 16052
724-865-9371

Daubenspeck's Orchard
592 Fairview Road
Petrolia, PA 16050
724-894-2824

Deener's Farm Market
21255 Perry Highway, Route 19
Cranberry Township, PA 16066
724-452-7944

Harvest Valley Farms
130 Ida Lane
Valencia, PA 16059
724-443-3558
www.harvestvalleyfarms.com

Hawkins Farm Market
409 Route 228
Valencia, PA 16059
724-625-1211

Henrick's Farm
227 Centreville Pike
Slippery Rock, PA 16057
724-794-8668

Kerr's Greenhouse
2900 Old Route 422 East
Fenelton, PA 16034
724-282-1275

Metrick's Harvest View Farm
143 Eagle Mill Road
Butler, PA 16001
724-282-8038

Natili Farm Market
Route 108
Slippery Rock, PA 16057
724-794-8823

Naylor's Orchard
Route 8
Cooperstown, PA 16059
724-486-2647

Pajer Farm Market
238 Ekastown Road
Sarver, PA 16055
724-353-1577

Sally's Cider Press
465 Perry Highway
Harmony, PA 16037
724-452-4545

Schramm Grower and Marketer
291 Crisswell Road
Butler, PA 16001
724-282-3714

Shirey's Farm Markets and Greenhouse
947 New Castle Road
Slippery Rock, PA 16057
724-637-2032

*Snyder's Farm
152 Snyder Lane
Chicora, PA 16025
724-445-3116

Taylor's Farm and Market
Route 8
Harrisville, PA 16038
724-735-2673

Zang's Greenhouse
396 Saxonburg Road
Butler, PA 16001
724-282-8125

Cambria County

A Bee Company
R.D. 1
Hastings, PA 16646
814-247-9934

Hite Farms
385 Eckenrode Mill Road
Patton, PA 16668
814-674-8656

Kamaw Open Air Market
2704 Glendale Valley Boulevard
Flinton, PA 16640
814-687-4233

Pat Leiden Farm
227 Leiden Lane
Patton, PA 16668
814-674-8464

Shevock Orchard
267 Betz Road
Sidman, PA 15955
814-495-4618

Sweet Water Farm
157 Sutton Lane
Loretto, PA 15940
814-886-9254

Vale Wood Farms
P.O. Box 203
Cresson, PA 16630
814-886-7171
www.valewoodfarms.com

Cameron County

James R. Zoschg, Sr.
HCR 03
Emporium, PA 15834
814-486-0705

Carbon County

Cressley's Greenhouse
and Produce Farm
4026 Long Run Road
Lehighton, PA 18235
610-377-1629

*Graver Orchards
1600 Owl Creek Road
Lehighton, PA 18235
610-377-0769

Mahoning Farmers' Market
2522 Blakeslee Road
Lehighton, PA 18235
570-386-2329

Merkel Farm and Nursery
209 Washington Road
Lehighton, PA 18235
570-386-4828

Semmel Farm
1146 West Lizard Creek Road
Lehighton, PA 18235
610-377-1189

Walker's Tree Farm
308 Spruce Street
Lehighton, PA 18235
610-377-1829

Centre County

Bayer's Mt. Honey
and Beeswax Crafts
R.D. 3
Tyrone, PA 16686
814-684-1783

Glick's Custom Woodwork and
Greenhouse
R.D. 2
Howard, PA 16841

Greenhouse on Rock Road
100 Rock Road
State College, PA 16801
814-238-0479

Harner Farm
2191 West Whitehall Road
State College, PA 16801
814-237-7919

Hollis Garden Center
and Greenhouse Nursery
R.R. 3
Philipsburg, PA 16866
814-339-6289

Kerstetter's Market
907 Nittany Valley Drive
Bellefonte, PA 16823
814-383-4459

MacNeal's Orchards
and Sugarbush
HCR 1
Rebersburg, PA 16872
814-349-8966

Mothersbaugh Farm
R.D. 2
Spring Mills, PA 16875
814-364-9482

Mountain Home Farm
R.D. 1, 605 Sengle Lane
Julian, PA 16844
814-355-2655

Patchwork Farm
R.D. 1
Aaronsburg, PA 16820
814-422-8735

Plum Grove Gardens
297 Plum Grove Lane
Julian, PA 16844
814-355-2267

Way Fruit Farm
R.D. 3
Port Matilda, PA 16870
814-692-5211

White's Farm Produce
R.D. 2, Route 192
Centre Hall, PA 16828
814-364-1108

Chester County

Barnard's Orchard
1079 Wawaset Road
Kennett Square, PA 19348
610-347-2151

Duncan's Farm
966 Valley Forge Road
Devon, PA 19333
610-688-2786

Fox Meadow Farm
1439 Clover Mill Road
Chester Springs, PA 19425
610-827-9731

Glen Willow Orchards
1657 Glen Willow Road
Avondale, PA 19311
610-268-8743

*Highland Orchards
1000 Thorndale Road
West Chester, PA 19380
610-269-3494

Kennett Farms
326 East Hillendale Road
Kennett Square, PA 19348
610-444-9619

Milky Way Farm
521 Uwchlan Avenue
Chester Springs, PA 19425
610-827-1484
www.milkywayfarm.com

Northbrook Orchards
6 Northbrook Road
West Chester, PA 19382
610-793-1210

Pete's Produce Farm
1225 East Street Road
Westtown, PA 19395
610-399-3711

Quail Creek Farm
621 Newark Road
Landenberg, PA 19350
610-268-3258

SIW Vegetables, Hill Girt Farm
4317 South Creek Road
Chadds Ford, PA 19317
215-388-0656

Todd Road Produce
115 Todd Road
Honey Brook, PA 19344

Vollmecke Orchards
and Farm Market
155 Cedar Knoll Road
Coatesville, PA 19320
610-383-4616

Wynnorr Farm, Stratton's
Farm Market
1635 East Street Road
Glen Mills, PA 19342
610-399-9080

Yeager's Farm and Market
Route 113 and Western Road
Kimberton, PA 19442
610-935-8244

Clarion County

Fescemyer Farms
521 Burgoon Road
Summerville, PA 15864
814-379-3721

Fred's Vegetable Patch
R.R. 1
Lucinda, PA 16235
814-354-2875

Hillside Gardens
1452 Limestone Road
Summerville, PA 15864
814-764-5476

North Forty Farm
Clarion Town Square
Shippenville, PA 16254
814-354-6218

Pheasant Run Farm
R.R. 3
Emlenton, PA 16373
814-358-2657

Saylor's Farm Products
R.D. 1
Sligo, PA 16255
814-745-2306
www.saylorsfarm.com

Sensenig's Produce
R.D. 3
New Bethlehem, PA 16242
814-745-3375

Wingard's Farm Market
and Greenhouse
R.D. 1
Shippenville, PA 16254
814-782-3989

Zacherl's Farm Market
R.D. 2
Shippenville, PA 16254
814-226-9497

Clearfield County

Aletta's Farm Market
R.D. 3
Curwensville, PA 16833
814-236-2029

Dunzik-Krasinski Farms
R.D. 1
Morrisdale, PA 16858
814-345-5981

Mom and Pop Farm
P.O. Box 192
Smokerun, PA 16681
814-378-5160

Shaggy Meadows
R.D. 1
Luthersburg, PA 15848
814-583-5270
www.geocities.com/shaggy meadows/index.html

Sperfslage's Farm Market
P.O. Box 46
Drifting, PA 16834
814-345-5359

Clinton County

East End Greenhouse and Produce
R.D. 1
Mill Hall, PA 17751

Pozy Heaven
R.R. 1
Jersey Shore, PA 17740
570-753-5513

River Farm Market
HCR 80
Lock Haven, PA 17745
570-748-6469

Wendell B. Coy
R.D. 2
Lock Haven, PA 17745
570-748-5047

Columbia County

Cole's PA Century Farm
R.R. 4
Benton, PA 17814
570-925-6907

Diehl's Farm Market
R.R. 9
Bloomsburg, PA 17815
570-437-3713

Fester Ridge Farm Market
R.R. 2
Berwick, PA 18603
570-752-5064

Kemmerer's Farm Market
7185 New Berwick Highway
Bloomsburg, PA 17815
570-752-7220

Kessler and Sons Orchards
R.R. 4
Berwick, PA 18603
570-752-7715

Kline's Pumpkin Express
R.R. 4
Benton, PA 17814
570-925-6173

Klinger's Plants-N-Produce
R.R. 3
Catawissa, PA 17820
570-799-5315

Krums Orchards and Farm Market
R.R. 2
Catawissa, PA 17820
570-356-2329

Morning Dew Produce
2100 West Front Street
Berwick, PA 18603
570-759-1260

Rohrbach's Farm Market and Gift Shop
R.D. 3
Catawissa, PA 17820
570-356-7654

Seholtz Greenhouses and Garden Center
6820 Keffer's Lane
Bloomsburg, PA 17815
570-784-5982

Shelhamer Farms
R.D. 2
Berwick, PA 18603
570-683-5239

Crawford County

Al's Melon Farm
6340 Harmonsburg Road
Linesville, PA 16424
814-683-4121

Ammen Miller
R.D. 1
Atlantic, PA 16111

Burgess Farm
R.D. 2
Springboro, PA 16435
814-587-2312

Getty Farm and Store
23394 Gravel Run Road
Saegertown, PA 16433
814-398-4700

Hickory Grove Orchard
and Cider Mill
2341 Fries Road
Espyville, PA 16424
724-927-6500

Jack Finney Farm
24999 Highway 99
Cambridge Springs, PA 16403
814-398-4590

Maple Hollow Farm
R.D. 2
Cambridge Springs, PA 16403
814-398-2607

Martin's Farm Market
13101 Putman Road
Conneaut Lake, PA 16316
814-382-6657

Meadville Market House
910 Market Street
Meadville, PA 16335
814-336-2056

Miller's Greenhouse
and Truck Patch
22674 Highway 27
Meadville, PA 16335
814-333-6312

Pavlicek Small Time Orchards
R.D. 2, Route 19 South
Cochranton, PA 16344
814-425-7721

Sclabach's Dutch Bakery
987 Milledgeville Road
Cochranton, PA 16314
724-253-2379

Swartzentruber's Farm Market
R.R. 1
Atlantic, PA 16111

Cumberland County

Ashcombe Farm and Greenhouses
906 Grantham Road
Mechanicsburg, PA 17055
717-766-7611

Bates Farm Market
1632 York Road
Carlisle, PA 17013
717-258-6522

C & S Produce
1122 Enola Road
Newburg, PA 17240

Deitch's Farm Market
1102 Mount Road
Newburg, PA 17240
717-423-5548

Derick Orchards
R.D. 1
Newburg, PA 17240
717-423-5232

Hillside Farm Market
18809 Spring Run Road
Spring Run, PA 17262

The Lloyds'
1724 Walnut Bottom Road
Newville, PA 17241
717-776-5730

Meadowbrook Produce
1022 Park Place
Mechanicsburg, PA 17055
717-258-6220

Mountain Lakes Farm Market
298 McAllister Church Road
Carlisle, PA 17013
717-243-9251

Mountain View Nursery
1101 Park Place
Mechanicsburg, PA 17055
717-766-4966

Musser Farm Market
Oldstone House Road
and Route 641
Carlisle, PA 17013
717-766-2367

Myer's Farm Market
1369 Creek Road
Boiling Spring, PA 17007
717-258-3893

Nolt's Farm Fresh Produce
7935 White Church Road
Shippensburg, PA 17257
717-530-1418

Paulus Farm Market
1216 South York Road
Mechanicsburg, PA 17055
717-766-8811
www.paulusfarmmarket.com

Strock's Farm Fresh Meats
729 Williams Grove Road
Mechanicsburg, PA 17055
717-697-2824

Toigo Orchards
750 South Mt. Estate Road
Shippensburg, PA 17257
717-532-4655

Dauphin County

Broad Street Market
1233 North 3rd Street
Harrisburg, PA 17105
717-236-7923
www.broadstmarket.com

Chester Schwartz
278 Pond Road
Hegins, PA 17048
717-365-3218

Kline Village Shopping Center
Farmers' Market
101 South 25th and Market Streets
Harrisburg, PA 17101
717-255-9560

Little Spring Trout Lake
3511 Fishing Creek Valley Road
Harrisburg, PA 17112
717-599-5565

Red Hill Farm
3641 Engle Road
Middletown, PA 17057
717-367-2052

Schwartz Farms
278 Pond Road
Lykens, PA 17048
717-365-3218

Spring Brook Farm
3475 Peters Mountain Road
Halifax, PA 17032

Strite's Orchards
1000 Strite's Road
Harrisburg, PA 17111
717-564-3130
www.striteorchard.com

Delaware County

Indian Orchards
24 Copes Lane
Media, PA 19063
610-565-8387

*Linvilla Orchards
137 West Knowlton Road
Media, PA 19063
610-876-7116
www.linvilla.com

Rittenhouse Farms
389 Lancaster Avenue
Strafford, PA 19087
610-687-3156

Wolff's Apple House
81 South Pennell Road
Lima, PA 19037
610-566-1680

Elk County

Green Acres
516 Hall Avenue
St. Marys, PA 15857
814-781-6627

Karen's Country Farm Market
and Greenhouse
R.D. 1, Montmorenci Road
Ridgway, PA 15853

Swiss Rifle Club Farm
R.D. 1
Ridgway, PA 15853
814-772-0210

Valley Farm Market
Route 255
Weedville, PA 15868
814-787-8911

Erie County

*Arundale Farm and Cider Mill
11731 East Main Street
North East, PA 16428
814-725-1079

*Boyce Fruit Farm
6590 Meadville Road
Girard, PA 16417
814-774-4778

Burdick's Farm Market
Route 18
Girard, PA 16417
814-774-4172

Chace Farm
11555 East Middle Road
North East, PA 16428
814-725-5309

Claron Farms
11312 Route 97
Waterford, PA 16441
814-796-4542

Corry Farmers' Market
19 North Center Street
Corry, PA 16047
814-665-9925

Erickson Farms
9813 Drury Road
Girard, PA 16417
814-774-8121

Finnell Farms
7840 Buffalo Road
Harborcreek, PA 16421
814-899-7187

Frank's Farm Market
5880 Sterrettania Road
Fairview, PA 16415
814-833-7230

Gardner Produce
12441 Draketown Road
Edinboro, PA 16412
814-734-3776

Goodwin's Farm Market
4115 Old French Road
Erie, PA 16504
814-864-7276

Hirtzel Farm
1740 Hirtzel Road
North East, PA 16428
814-725-5096

Holliday's Crooked Creek Farm
455 Holliday Road
North Springfield, PA 16430
814-922-3517

*Kruse Farms
6911 West Lake Road
Fairview, PA 16415
814-474-3095

Langdon's Farm Market
Route 20
Harborcreek, PA 16421
814-899-6863

Lehman Farms
6600 Lexington Road
Girard, PA 16417
814-774-2139

Luke Farm
7374 Belle Road
Harborcreek, PA 16421
814-899-5123

Maple Row Farm
4561 Williams Road
Girard, PA 16417
814-774-2118

Mason Farms Country Market
839 Peninsula Drive
Erie, PA 16505
814-833-9933

Mobilia Fruit Farm
12234 Archer Road
North East, PA 16428
814-725-4077

Nelson Fruit Farm
7931 East Lake Drive
Erie, PA 16511
814-899-6240

Paul Pangratz Farm
5210 Daggett Road
Girard, PA 16417
814-774-4448

Rassie Farms
8259 Singer Road
North East, PA 16428
814-725-2192

Richter Farms
6400 Firman Road
Erie, PA 16510
814-898-4113

Sandy Acre Farm
9377 West Lake Road
Erie, PA 16501

*Sceiford Farms
611 Dwey Road
North East, PA 16428
814-725-1492

*Trocki Farms
Route 89
North East, PA 16428
814-725-1068

Wasielewski Farms
8740 Hamot Road
Waterford, PA 16441
814-866-9793

Wiser's Fruit and Vegetable Farm
9037 Ridge Road
Girard, PA 16417
570-622-2337

Wooden Nickel Buffalo Farm
5970 Koman Road
Edinboro, PA 16412
814-734-2833

Fayette County

Cavanaugh Greenhouse
R.D. 1
East Millsboro, PA 15433
724-785-2860

Herrington's Greenhouse
Corner of Routes 119 and 982
Connellsville, PA 15425
724-628-7993

Kujawa's Farm
R.D. 1, 104 Sherrick Road
Connellsville, PA 15425
724-626-0648

Laurel Highland Nurseries
2060 Morgantown Road,
Route 119 South
Uniontown, PA 15401
724-437-6867

Rich Farms
R.D. 1, Route 857
Smithfield, PA 15478
724-564-7644

Forest County

Pleasant Valley Farm
R.R. 1
Tionesta, PA 16355
814-755-3911

Franklin County

Bingaman's Farm Market
14120 Williamsport Pike
Greencastle, PA 17225
717-597-5555

Bingham's Orchard and Market
9823 Lincoln Highway West
St. Thomas, PA 17252
717-369-2218

Blue Mountain Farm
8543 McClays Mill Road
Newburg, PA 17240
717-532-5537

Breezy Valley Farm
and Greenhouses
15798 Cumberland Highway
Newburg, PA 17240
717-532-5070

*Country Acres
2413 Country Road
Chambersburg, PA 17201
717-263-2918

Donald Hess Orchard
5355 Hess Benedict Road
Waynesboro, PA 17268
717-762-4151

Etter's Roadside Produce
5167 Old Scotland Road
Shippensburg, PA 17257
717-263-3783

Granny's Garden Farm Market
7404 Anthony Highway
Waynesboro, PA 17268
717-677-8842

Guilford Gardens
4140 Church Road
Chambersburg, PA 17201
717-261-1700

Harold A. Boyer
6143 Cumberland Highway
Chambersburg, PA 17201
717-263-4818

Isaac W. Horst Orchards
11132 Tanyard Hill Road
Orrstown, PA 17244
717-532-2842

Jim's Country Market
25 Grant Street
Chambersburg, PA 17210
717-264-1273

*John Dehartog Orchard
2449 Hafer Road
Fayetteville, PA 17222
717-264-7397

Paul's Country Market
6374 Nunnery Road
Waynesboro, PA 17268
717-762-4840

Reynolds Farm
11129 Gehr Road
Waynesboro, PA 17268
717-762-2986

Shatzer Fruit Market
2197 Lincoln Way West/Route 30
Chambersburg, PA 17201
717-263-2195

Shindle's Orchard
6072 Valley Camp Road
Greencastle, PA 17225
717-369-3331

Trayer's Greenhouses
and Farm Market
11452 Welsh Run Road
Mercersburg, PA 17236
717-328-2456

Valley Road Produce
17597 Path Valley Road
Spring Run, PA 17262

Fulton County

J & E Kimball Crawford–New
Morning Farm
HCR 71
Hustontown, PA 17229
814-448-3904

Uncle Clem's Place
1158 Trails End Road
Harrisonville, PA 17228
717-485-9314

Greene County

Chessie's Market
R.R. 1
Carmichaels, PA 15320
724-966-5414

Greene County Produce
R.D. 4
Waynesboro, PA 15370

Little Greene Apples Farm Market
R.D. 5
Waynesboro, PA 15370
724-852-2259

Huntingdon County

Cedar Hill Farm
HC 01
Spruce Creek, PA 16683
814-632-8319

Durbin Farms Market
R.D. 4
Tyrone, PA 16686
814-632-6255

Huntingdon Farmers' Market
Route 22
Huntingdon, PA 16652
814-627-6122

Leidig's Farm
R.D. 4
Tyrone, PA 16686
814-632-6986

Log Cabin Farmers' Market
Route 22
Huntingdon, PA 16652
814-793-9379

New Leaf Farm
R.D. 1
Warriors Mark, PA 16877
814-632-5378

Indiana County

Autumn House Farm
R.D. 1
Rochester Mill, PA 15771
724-286-9596
www.autumnhousefarm.com

Berry Hill of Stutzman Farms
R.D. 1
Penn Run, PA 15765
724-463-9350

Brookdale Farm
R.D. 3
Homer City, PA 15748
724-479-2762

Clearview Farms
Behm Road
Rochester Mill, PA 15771
724-286-9129

Hill's Orchard
R.D. 1
Rochester Mill, PA 15771
724-286-9546

Olliver's Vegetable Farm
R.D. 1
Saltsburg, PA 15681
724-639-3965

Pappie's Plants and Produce
R.D. 2
Indiana, PA 15701
724-354-2642

Reeger's Vegetable Farm
755 Laurel Road
Shelocta, PA 15774
724-463-0440

Silverbrook Meadows/Shop/
Heritage Tours
16040 U.S. Highway 119 North
Marchland, PA 15758
724-286-3317 or 800-208-3082

Yarnick's Farm
R.D. 2
Indiana, PA 15701
724-349-3904

Jefferson County

Bennett Farms and Greenhouse
R.D. 3
Reynoldsville, PA 15851
814-427-5276

Cooper Farm Market
R.D. 1
Falls Creek, PA 15840
814-371-2239

Country Living Center
R.D. 2
Reynoldsville, PA 15851
814-653-8646

Himes Farms
R.D. 1
Reynoldsville, PA 15851
814-653-9529

James Whitesell
R.R. 5
Punxsutawney, PA 15767
814-938-5788

Seigworth Farm Market
R.D. 4
Brookville, PA 15825
814-849-7060

Juniata County

Happy Breeze Farm
R.R. 2, Butchershop Road
Port Royal, PA 17082
717-527-4081

Kanagy Produce
R.D. 3
Mifflintown, PA 17059

Sharp's Orchard and Farm Market
HCR 63
Mifflintown, PA 17059
717-436-8191

Tuscarora Mountain Acres
R.R. 1
Honey Grove, PA 17035
717-734-3745

Lackawanna County

Abington Farmers' Market
12055 Rose Drive
Clarks Summit, PA 18411
570-587-0391

D & W Farm Market
2345 Milwaukee Road
Clarks Summit, PA 18411
570-587-5638

Grist Mill Hill Farm
R.D. 1
Dalton, PA 18414
570-563-2322

Highland Farm
R.D. 2
Dalton, PA 18414
570-587-0002

Ken Rees
Dean Road
Dalton, PA 18414
570-563-1067

Landsiedel's Pumpkin Patch
126016 Airport Drive
Dalton, PA 18414
570-587-1854

Ledge Hill Farms
R.R. 3, Ross Road
Dalton, PA 18414
570-378-2212

Miller Farm/Cat-O-Nine Tails Farm
Sunset Drive
Laplume, PA 18440
570-945-3000

Miller's Orchard Farm Market
1515 Fairview Road
Clarks Summit, PA 18411
570-586-3399

Mountain Road Farm
900 Barring Avenue
Scranton, PA 18501
570-586-9503

Pullman Farms
1511 Summit Lake Road
Summit, PA 18411
570-587-3258

Ritter's Cider Mill
I-84 Exit/Wimmer's Road
Lake Ariel, PA 18436
570-689-9790

Rosenkran's Farm
Scranton, Morgan Highway
and Keyser Avenue Junction
Falls, PA 18615
570-378-3567

Valley View Farm
13019 Valley View Drive
Clarks Summit, PA 18411
570-587-5251

Lancaster County

Blue Gate Produce and Bake Shop
2725A Lincoln Highway East
Ronks, PA 17572

Cedar Meadow Farm
679 Hilldale Road
Holtwood, PA 17532

Cherry Hill Orchards Outlet
2183 New Danville Pike
Lancaster, PA 17603
717-872-9311

Country Farm Market
708 Strasburg Pike
Lancaster, PA 17602

David Fisher Farm
2828 Lincoln Highway East
Ronks, PA 17572

Elam S. Beiler
5645 Umbletown Road
Gap, PA 17527

Elm Road Produce
211 Elm Road
Lititz, PA 17543

Elmer Stoltzfus
171 Quarry Road
Leola, PA 17540
717-656-2120

Fahnestock Fruit Farm
198 Fairview Road
Lititz, PA 17543
717-665-7764

FDR Produce
407 Hilltop Road
Strasburg, PA 17579
717-687-7288

Funk's Farm Market
and Garden Center
306 South Duke Street
Millersville, PA 17551
717-872-8411

Gideon F. Stoltzfus
561 White Horse Road
Gap, PA 17527
717-442-4406

Hampshire Orchard
1813 Camp Road
Manheim, PA 17545
717-664-3343

Hilltop Acres Farm Market
347 Rife Run Road
Manheim, PA 17545
717-665-7809

Hitz Farm Market
2684 Lebanon Road
Manheim, PA 17545
717-664-2922

Hottenstein's Farm Market
and Bakery
1900 State Road
Lancaster, PA 17601
717-898-7021

Jacob S. Stoltzfus
39 Colonial Road
Gordonville, PA 17529

Kauffman's Farm Market
1619 Geogetown Road
Christiana, PA 17509

Kauffman's Fruit Farm and Market
3097 Old Philadelphia Pike
Bird in Hand, PA 17505
717-768-7112

Lapp Valley Farm
244 Mentzer Road
New Holland, PA 17557
717-354-7988

Neustadter and Zimmerman
448 Mt. Sidney Road
Witmer, PA 17585
717-393-1658

Nolt's Produce
577 Warehouse Road
Manheim, PA 17545
717-665-6614

Peach Lane Produce
91 East Whiteoak Road
Ronks, PA 17572

Red Barn Farm Market
1402 Georgetown Road
Quarryville, PA 17566
717-529-6040

Rohrer Family Farm
2651 Oregon Pike
Lititz, PA 17543
717-569-7929

Root's Country Market
and Auction
705 Graystone Road
Manheim, PA 17545
717-898-7811

Schantz Farm
606 Springville Road
Ephrata, PA 17522
717-733-2900

Schopf Brothers Farm Market
3493 Marietta Avenue
Lancaster, PA 17601
717-285-7748

Shenk's
1980 New Danville Pike
Lancaster, PA 17603
717-393-4240
www.shenks.com

Shuman's Produce
547 Donerville Road
Lancaster, PA 17603
717-872-2596

Summit Hill Produce
101 Summit Hill Drive
Paradise, PA 17562
717-687-6068

Weavers Orchard
797 Old Line Road
Manheim, PA 17545
717-664-4454

Windy Hill Farm
993 Holly Tree Road
Manheim, PA 17545
717-665-3803

Zimmerman Orchard
1879 Main Street
East Earl, PA 17519
717-445-5526

Lawrence County

Apple Castle
New Castle Sharon Road
New Wilmington, PA 16142
724-652-3221

Bordonaros Fruitland Market
305 Neal Street
New Castle, PA 16101

Miller's Market
Route 956, 1 mile south
of New Wilmington
New Castle, PA 16105
724-946-2896

*Quarry Lake Orchard
Nashua Road
New Castle, PA 16105
724-654-4888

Lebanon County

David M. Kreider
2709 Tunnel Hill Road
Lebanon, PA 17046
717-272-8501

Hitz Farm Market in the Tent
Route 422
Annville, PA 17003
717-867-2074

Honey Bear Orchards
1819 Thompson Avenue
Lebanon, PA 17046
717-867-4611

Hopedale Farm
Route 443 East
Grantville, PA 17028
717-469-7704

Limestone Springs
930 Tulpehocken Road
Richland, PA 17087
717-866-2461

Mountain Hollow Farm
289 West Texter Mission Road
Robesonia, PA 19551
610-589-2169

Musser's Produce
2251 South Lincoln Avenue
Lebanon, PA 17046
717-273-3070

R and R Orchards
951 Houtztown Road
Myerstown, PA 17067
717-933-8337

Risser-Marvel Farm Market
2425 Horseshoe Pike
Annville, PA 17003
717-838-1438

Sycamore Spring Orchard
2501 Heilmandale Road
Jonestown, PA 17038
717-867-4389

White Birch Farm
R.D. 4, Route 322
Lebanon, PA 17042
717-867-1034

Lehigh County

Billig's Fruit and Vegetables
8263 Allemaengel Road (Route 863)
New Tripoli, PA 18066
610-298-2862

Brookvue Farms
26 Brookvue Lane
Mertztown, PA 19539
610-682-2330

Clearview Farm
3041 Old Post Road
Slatington, PA 18080
610-767-2049

County Line Orchard
9200 Kings Highway
Kempton, PA 19529
610-756-6411

Crystal Spring Farm
355 Bellview Road
Schnecksville, PA 18078
610-799-4611

Eagle Point Farm
Route 100
Trexlertown, PA 18087
610-395-8620

Fritchey Farms
East Grant Street
Slatedale, PA 18079
610-767-8304

Grim's Greenhouse
and Farm Market
9941 Schantz Road
Breinigsville, PA 18031
610-395-5655

Hausman's Fruit Farm
2915 Limeport Pike
Coopersburg, PA 18036
610-967-2440

Hometown Farm Market
553 North 4th Street
Allentown, PA 18102

Marbo Farms
6145 Weaversville Road
Bethlehem, PA 18017
610-264-4267

Pine Brook Hollow Tree Farm
4301 East Macungie Road
Emmaus, PA 18049
610-966-3748

Prydenjoy Farm
2141 Pirma Avenue
Allentown, PA 18104
610-433-8826

Red Cat Farm
6113 Memorial Road
Germansville, PA 18053
610-767-2519

Ringer's Market
4029 Mauch Chunk Road
Coplay, PA 18037
610-799-3164

Sheepy Hollow Farm
4750 Churchview Road
Zionsville, PA 18092
610-967-3175

Shoemaker's Orchard
7503 Kernsville Road
Orefield, PA 18069
610-395-9598

Shuman's Orchard
7059 Elementary Road
Coopersburg, PA 18036
610-967-2690

Spring Hollow Farm
3480 Moyer Court
New Tripoli, PA 18066
610-285-2066

Stonehouse Farms
4698 North Church Road
Egypt, PA 18052
610-261-1084

Suyundalla Farms
1848 Clearview Road
Coplay, PA 18037
610-261-9098

True Life Family Acres
4315 Washington Street
Schnecksville, PA 18078
610-767-5433

Luzerne County

Brace's Orchard
R.D. 3, Brace Road
Dallas, PA 18612
570-333-4236

Broyan's Farm Produce
R.R. 1, East Zenith Road
Nescopeck, PA 18635
570-379-3286

Charney Farms
R.R. 1, Pecks Road
Harding, PA 18643
570-388-2155

Dagostin Orchard
2 miles west of Route 93
Sugarloaf, PA 18249
570-788-1806

Dymond's Farm and Farm Market
R.D. 3, Brace Road
Dallas, PA 18612

Dymond's Farm Market and Bakery
251 North Memorial Highway
Shavertown, PA 18708
570-675-1696

Golomb's Farm and Greenhouse
60 McCullough Road
Plains, PA 18705
570-825-4072

Larry and Bob O'Malia Farm Market
125 North River Street
Plains, PA 18702
570-822-3805

Lewis Orchard
R.R. 4
Harding, PA 18643
570-388-6927

Martin O'Malia Farmers' Market
747 North Main Street
Plains, PA 18705
570-824-0490

Norman Darling Farms
and Greenhouses
356 A Hildebrandt Road
Dallas, PA 18612
570-675-2080

Pumpkinhill Produce Farms
250 Wapwallopen Road, Route 239
Nescopeck, PA 18635
570-379-2106

Spencer's Strawberry Farm
and Apple Orchard
315 Huntsville Road
Shavertown, PA 18708
570-779-1253

Windy Hill Farm
Lewis Road
Wyoming, PA 18644

Lycoming County

Beech Grove Farm
3410 Route 184
Trout Run, PA 17771
570-634-3197

Beiler Farm
752 Elimsport Road
Montgomery, PA 17752

Bruce Frymire
415 South Howard Street
South Williamsport, PA 17701
570-323-0400

Dick Tebbs Farms
1620 Four Mile Drive
Williamsport, PA 17701
570-323-7638

Enders Fruit Farm
68 Orchard Lane
Jersey Shore, PA 17740
570-745-7783

Friendly Farmers' Market
Route 44 South to Route 880 South,
1 mile to Gotshall Road
Jersey Shore, PA 17740
570-745-2268

Johnson Mt. View Farm
Route 44
Collomsville, PA 17701

Lane's End Farm
Route 287 to Route 973, west 2 miles
Jersey Shore, PA 17740
570-398-2078

Lorson's Fruit Farm
Route 654, 10 miles to Breeze Inn,
turn left
Williamsport, PA 17701
570-745-7705

Paulings
Off Route 188, 2 1/2 miles east
of Hughesville
Hughesville, PA 17737
570-584-5502

Provident Farms
Near Route 15, 30 miles north
of Williamsport
Liberty, PA 16930
570-324-2285

Ralph Styer Farm
Off Route 405 at railroad, 1 mile
west of Muncy
Muncy, PA 17756
570-546-5706

Steinbecker Orchard
On Route 654, 7 miles west
of Williamsport
Williamsport, PA 17701
570-745-7532

Tom Styer Farm and Market
215 Shady Lane
Muncy, PA 17756
570-546-5861

Wentzler's Fruit Farm
Lycoming Mall exit of Route 220,
left at light
Muncy, PA 17756
570-546-5574

McKean County

Rocky Ridge Orchards
South Settlement Road
Kane, PA 16735
814-837-8850

Mercer County

Bortz's Orchard
549 Mercer Road
Greenville, PA 16125
724-588-2688

Cantaberry Acres
152 Nutt Road
Grove City, PA 16127
814-786-8355

Cresswel's Farm Market
847 North Perry Highway
Mercer, PA 16137
724-475-3551

Dutch Lane Farm Market
Coolspring Church Road
Mercer, PA 16137
724-475-3792

Farm Fresh Products
69 McCartney Road
Fredonia, PA 16124

Joe's Greenhouse
and Farm Market
2265 River Road
Hermitage, PA 16146
724-962-5511

Kepner's Produce
3713B Sandy Lake Road
Sandy Lake, PA 16145
724-376-2483

Mozes Fruit and Vegetables
320 Cherry Hill Road
Greenville, PA 16125
724-588-9480

Ryglewiczs' Farm and Greenhouse
251 Old Ash Road
Mercer, PA 16137
724-748-4424

Seiver's Farm Market
911 West Main Street
Grove City, PA 16127
724-458-7719

Shirley Taylor
2540 Butler Pike
Grove City, PA 16127

Veg-Acres Farm
and Greenhouse
374 Dowling Road
Jamestown, PA 16134
724-932-3776

Mifflin County

Aurand's
1385 Big Ridge Road
Lewistown, PA 17044
717-248-7688

Esh's Orchard
10744 Back Mountain Orchard
Milroy, PA 17063
717-677-2606

Golden Mile Farmers' Market
1385 Big Ridge Road
Lewistown, PA 17044
717-677-2606

McNitt's Apple Place
10 Apple Place Lane
Milroy, PA 17063
717-667-3873

Overmeyer's Orchard
68 East Juniata Drive
Mount Union, PA 17066
814-542-4290

Monroe County

Brookside Gardens
Off Route 209 on West Hills Road
Stroudsburg, PA 18360
570-421-7235

Gould's Produce and Farm Market
Frable Road
Brodheadsville, PA 18322
570-992-5615

Heckman Orchards
On Route 115, 4 miles north
of Brodheadsville
Effort, PA 18330
570-629-1191

Seidof's
On Route 209, 2 miles west
of Sciota
Sciota, PA 18354
570-992-4611

Smale's Farm Store
On Route 534, 3 miles west
of Kresgeville
Jonas, PA 18058
570-629-2493

Montgomery County

Dull's Farm
1001 Limekiln Pike
Ambler, PA 19002
215-646-6951

Frankenfield Farm
98 Allentown Road
Elroy, PA 18964
215-723-3906

Freddy Hill Farms
1440 Sumneytown Pike
Lansdale, PA 19446
215-855-1205

Grindleton
Grindleton Lane
Ambler, PA 19002
215-646-7760

Henry Garges
843 Harleysville Pike
Harleysville, PA 19438
215-256-9917

Kohler Farms
1262 Limekiln Pike
Ambler, PA 19002
215-646-4941

Maple Acres Farm
2656 Narcissa Road
Plymouth Meeting, PA 19462
610-828-4953

Merrymead Farm
2222 Valley Forge Road
Lansdale, PA 19446
610-584-4410

Nicholas Giangiacomo
806 Collegeville Road
Collegeville, PA 19426
610-489-0126

Perkiomen Valley Orchard
2478 Perkiomenville Road
Harleysville, PA 19438
215-234-4323

Ringing Hill Orchards
1453 Bliem Road
Pottstown, PA 19464
610-326-0344

Stauffer Fruit Stand
Route 663
Pennsburg, PA 18073
215-679-5894

Varner's Tree Farm and Cider Mill
746 South Trappe Road, Route 113
Collegeville, PA 19426
610-489-8878

Zern's Farm Market
Route 73
Gilbertsville, PA 19525

Montour County

Siegrist's Greenhouses
and Produce Farm
On Sunbury-Elysburg Road,
6 miles east of Sunbury
Danville, PA 17821
570-672-3239

Northampton County

*Bayberry Orchards I
3611 Bayberry Drive
Danielsville, PA 18038
610-767-8574

Bayberry Orchards II
8545 Airport Road
Northampton, PA 18067
610-767-8574

Bechdolt Orchard
2209 Leithsville Road
Hellertown, PA 18055
610-838-8522

Becker Farms
262 Trapper Road
Northampton, PA 18067
610-262-6400

Elvern Farm Market
Bluevalley Drive
Bangor, PA 18013
610-588-6335

Heinsohn's Greenhouses
Farm Stand
Route 512 at Five Points
Bangor, PA 18013
610-588-5632

Indian Creek Farm
3479 Mango Drive
Danielsville, PA 18038
610-760-0739

Kessler Farms
6092 Sullivan Trail
Nazareth, PA 18064
610-759-2255

Sandt's Market
1021 Broadway
Windgap, PA 18091
610-863-9224

Seiple Farms
5761 Nor-Bath Blvd.
Bath, PA 18014
610-837-6282

Twin Maple Farms
7486 School Road
Bath, PA 18014
610-837-0175

Upstream Farm and Store
2601 Bushkill Drive
Easton, PA 18042
610-253-6450

Northumberland County

Dries Orchard
Off Route 890, 7 miles south of Sunbury
Sunbury, PA 17801
570-286-6723

George Stahl
On Mile Hill Road, 1 mile east of Sunbury
Sunbury, PA 17801
570-286-0089

K. Schlegel Farms
On Route 147, 1 mile south of Dalmatia
Dalmatia, PA 17017
570-758-2407

Sunbury Market House
434 Market Street
Sunbury, PA 17801
570-374-5503

Perry County

Butcher's Farm Market
4th Street to Fickes Lane, 3/4 mile north of Newport Square
Newport, PA 17074
717-567-9884

Hall's Farm Market and Bakery
4900 Spring Road
Shermansdale, PA 17090
717-582-7541

Philadelphia County

Dutch Country Farmers' Market
2031 Cottman Avenue
Philadelphia, PA 19149
215-745-6008

Firehouse Farmers' Market
703 South 50th Street
Philadelphia, PA 19143
215-729-4124

Kauffman Produce
12th and Filbert Streets
Philadelphia, PA 19107
215-592-1898

South and Passyunk Farmers' Market
318 Gaskill Street
Philadelphia, PA 19147
215-925-5971

Potter County

Mitchell's Twin Valley Market
175 South Mitchell Road
Galeton, PA 16922
814-435-8276

Prouty Trout Farm
971 Prouty Road
Austin, PA 16720
814-647-8474

Raven Hill and Mountain Produce
421 Raven Hill Road
Roulette, PA 16746
814-544-7352

Thorny Bush Farm
Coudersport Courthouse Square
Coudersport, PA 16915
814-274-0504

Schuylkill County

Anderson Farms
1113 Long Run Road
Friedensburg, PA 17933

B & R Farms
Ringtown-Shenandoah Highway
Ringtown, PA 17967
570-889-3197

Blyler Fruit Farm
7922 Route 25
Spring Glen, PA 17978
570-365-3177

Leiby's Farm Market
Catawissa Road in Lewistown Valley
Tamaqua, PA 18252
570-668-3258

Pine Creek Country Gardens
Route 443
Friedensburg, PA 17933
570-739-1140

Rodichok's Farm Market
200 Wisconisco Avenue
Tower City, PA 17980
570-647-9492

Stein's Farm Market
R.D. 1
Orwigsburg, PA 17961
570-943-2375

W. C. Fields
R.D. 2
Orwigsburg, PA 17961
570-943-2211

Zukovich's Farm Market
Off Route 309, 1 mile west of Walt's Drive-In
Tamaqua, PA 18252
570-4672039

Snyder County

Brubakers Orchard
Off Route 104, 3 miles east of Penns Creek
Winfield, PA 17889
570-837-3735

522 Market
Route 522
Selinsgrove, PA 17870

Hazy Vale Farm
Chapman Road to Black Woods Road
Port Treverton, PA 17864
570-374-7267

*Joyful Acres
Route 522
Selinsgrove, PA 17870
570-374-7078

Middleburg Farmers' Market
Route 522
Middleburg, PA 17842
570-837-2222

Mitchell's Country Market
250 Main Street
Middleburg, PA 17842
570-837-1639

Mitterling's Fruit Farm
Route 35
Mount Pleasant Mills, PA 17853
570-539-8292

Suders Buckwheat Valley Produce and U-Pik Berries
Buckwheat Valley Road
Mount Pleasant Mills, PA 17853
570-539-2272

Sunny Side Farms
On Middlecreek Road, off Route 35
Selinsgrove, PA 17870
570-374-1777

Sweet Meriam's Farm
Markley Lane
Beaver Springs, PA 17812
570-658-8512

Swigart's Farm Market
Route 522
McClure, PA 17841
570-658-5125

Somerset County

Airesman Orchards
745 Edie Road
Somerset, PA 15501
814-445-5661

Allegheny Mountain Orchard
Route 160
Berlin, PA 15530
814-267-5282

Laurel Vista Farm
Bakersville-Edie Road in Allenvale
Somerset, PA 15501
814-443-2451

Milroy Farms
1724 River Road
Salisbury, PA 15558
814-662-4125

Sullivan County

The Greenery
Route 4008 in Estella
Forksville, PA 18616
570-924-4388

Sysocks Orchard
Route 87 North
Dushore, PA 18614
570-928-8613

Susquehanna County

Acre Long Farm
Route 92
Susquehanna, PA 18847
570-756-2635

Jayne's Orchards
R.D. 1
Laceyville, PA 18623
570-869-1405

Snug Hollow Farm
Route 547
Susquehanna, PA 18847
570-756-2697

Van Cott's Garden Center
Route 11
Hallstead, PA 18822
570-879-4740

Tioga County

The Barn Farm and Craft Market
1/4 mile northwest from Routes 6 and 660
Wellsboro, PA 16901
570-724-6984

Belz's Produce
R.D. 1
Tioga, PA 16946
570-835-5321

H & E Orchard
R.D. 1
Roaring Branch, PA 17765
570-673-8621

Jim and Dora Tice
427 Tice Road
Mainesburg, PA 16932
570-549-5257

Kichline's Backacre Farms
Route 3015, Welsh Settlement
Wellsboro, PA 16901
570-724-5284

Krystal Wharf Farms
7 miles northeast of Mansfield
Mansfield, PA 16933
570-549-5194

Mansfield Cider Mill
Route 6
Mansfield, PA 16933
570-662-2450

Owlett's Sunshine Farm Market
Route 287
Middlebury Center, PA 16935
570-376-2976

Union County

Anchor Farms
R.D. 1
New Columbia, PA 17856
570-538-1170

Ards Farm Market
Route 45
Lewisburg, PA 17837
570-524-9820

Maple Hill Farms
William Penn Drive at
Airport Road
Lewisburg, PA 17837
570-524-0791

Venango County

Eakin's Farm Market
Route 322 West
Cranberry, PA 16319

McCune's Produce
R.D. 1
Utica, PA 16362
814-425-3885

Pappy's Produce
250 Grant Street
Franklin, PA 16323
814-437-2089

Warren County

Cherry Grove Farms
1 mile east of Gregerson Road
Clarendon, PA 16313
814-968-3596

Olson's Fruit Farm
Cider Mill Hill Road
Russell, PA 16345
814-757-8347

Washington County

Bush's Farm Market
32 Bush Drive
Claysville, PA 15323
724-663-7344

Charleroi Farmers' Market
7th and Fallowfield
Charleroi, PA 15022
724-483-3507

Harden's Market
66 Wicheham Road
Fredericktown, PA 15333

Krenzelak Orchards
85 McCormick Lane
Prosperity, PA 15329
724-225-8761

Matthew's Farm and Greenhouse
116 Matthews Spur Road
Eighty Four, PA 15330
724-239-2118

McClelland's Farm Market
501B Galley Road
Canonsburg, PA 15317
724-745-4585

Rosefield Farm
297 Rural Valley Road
Claysville, PA 15323
724-948-3715

Simmon's Farm
170 Simmon's Road
McMurray, PA 15317
724-941-1490

Springhill Orchard
Kinder Road
Scenery Hill, PA 15360
724-945-5457

The Spring House
Box 112
Eighty Four, PA 15330
724-228-3339

Taggert's Orchard
184 Wotring Road
Washington, PA 15301
724-345-3656

*Tara Hill Orchard
273 Fort Cherry Road
McDonald, PA 15057
724-356-7624

Trax Farms
528 Trax Road
Finleyville, PA 15332
412-835-3246

Volkar Farm Market
Route 40 East
Richeyville, PA 15358
724-632-5877

Weatherbury Farm
1061 Sugar Run Road
Avella, PA 15312
724-587-3763

White Hall Farms
501 B Galley Road
Canonsburg, PA 15317
724-745-4585

Wayne County

Bertram's Orchard
Route 670
Honesdale, PA 18431
570-253-4105

Cavage's County Farmers' Market
Route 6
Honesdale, PA 18431
570-253-9036

Four Story Hill Farm
HC 62
Honesdale, PA 18431
570-224-4137

Klim's Orchard
Route 196
Lake Ariel, PA 18436
570-698-6981

North Slope Farm
Pleasant View Drive
Pleasant Mount, PA 18453
570-448-2374

Rush Mountain Organic Farm
Route 706
Montrose, PA 18801
570-278-9439

Westmoreland County

Chestnut Ridge Farms
R.R. 4
Latrobe, PA 15650
724-593-7041

Cokeville Produce Market
Route 217
Blairsville, PA 15717
724-459-9059

Comp's Farm
Kechsburg-Donegal Pike
Mount Pleasant, PA 15666
724-423-2541

Daugherty's Orchard and Greenhouses
5593 Saltsburg Road
Murrysville, PA 15668
724-327-1603

Hempfield Farmers' Market
Route 136
Greensburg, PA 15601
724-834-2334

Hyskell Farms
Route 819
Alverton, PA 15612
724-887-6389

J and K Produce
Route 982
Derry, PA 15627
724-539-3551

Ligonier Country Market
West Main Street
Ligonier, PA 15658

Mountain Produce
Route 31 East
Donegal, PA 15646
724-593-6805

Sarver's Hill Farm
R.R. 9
Greensburg, PA 15601

*Schramm Farms and Orchards
1002 Blank Road
Jeannette, PA 15644
724-744-7320

Simon's Orchard
2131 Route 819 North
Mount Pleasant, PA 15666
724-547-2406

Superior Produce Market
Route 22 East
New Alexandria, PA 15670
724-668-2144

Terri's Garden
R.R. 1
Smithton, PA 15479
724-872-4994

Uschock's Farm
Route 981
Greensburg, PA 15601
724-836-1631

Wyoming County

Denmon's Farm
R.R. 1
Noxen, PA 18636
570-298-2277

Grassy Ridge Farms
Route 29
Noxen, PA 18636
570-298-2377

Indian Oven Farm
Route 2
Falls, PA 18615
570-587-3437

The Petras Farm
1343 State Road 6 East
Tunkhannock, PA 18657
570-836-3495

Scholz's Orchards
Sugar Hollow Road
Mehoopany, PA 18629
570-833-2829

Trauger's Greenhouse
Scranton-Providence Road Exit
Factoryville, PA 18419
570-378-2561

Victor W. Decker
1119 Sugar Hollow Road
Tunkhannock, PA 18657
570-833-2486

York County

A. L. Brown and Son Orchard
R.D. 3
Spring Grove, PA 17362
717-225-1410

Barton's Farm Market
20199 Barrens Road South
Stewartstown, PA 17363
717-993-2494
www.bartonsfruitfarm.com

Belview Farm
1/2 mile off Route 851
New Park, PA 17352
717-382-4880

Bentzel's Orchard
21 North Lewisberry Road
Dillsburg, PA 17019
717-766-5160

Blevin's Fruit Farm
16222 West Liberty
Stewartstown, PA 17363
717-993-2885

Blueberry Hill
1870 Powder Mill Road
York, PA 17402
717-741-1003

Brown's Orchards and Farm Market
300 South Main Street
Loganville, PA 17342
717-428-2036
www.jarrettville.org/family/browns.htm

Central Market House
34 West Philadelphia and Beaver Streets
York, PA 17402
717-848-2243

Dale and Louise Wolf's Market
Route 234
East Berlin, PA 17316
717-259-9897

Davis' Farm Market
39 North York Road
Dillsburg, PA 17019
717-697-8152

Dennis Fitz Produce
2195 Springwood Road
York, PA 17403
717-843-1294

Fitz Brothers Farm Market
2670 Springwood Road
York, PA 17402
717-741-0246

*Goodling Farm Market
226 South Main Street
Loganville, PA 17342
717-428-2305

Hanson Farm Market
Richmond Road
Red Lion, PA 17356
717-927-9502

Houck's Country Market
128 Monument Road
York, PA 17403
717-741-2241

John Fitz Farm Market
510 Windsor Road
York, PA 17402
717-755-5729

Kenmar Farms
335 Indian Rock Dam Road
York, PA 17403
717-741-0708

*Maple Lawn Farms
251 East Maple Lawn Road
New Park, PA 17352
800-832-3697
www.maplelawnfarms.com

Mason Dixon Farm Market
18166 Susquehanna Trail
New Freedom, PA 17349
717-235-4338

Mowery Orchards
522 East Mount Airy Road
Dillsburg, PA 17019
717-766-4522

New Eastern Market
201 Memory Lane
York, PA 17402
717-755-5811

Paul and David Keeney Farm
194 Indian Rock Dam Road
York, PA 17403
717-741-1481

*Rinehart's Orchard and Farm Store
76 Mount Airy Road
Dillsburg, PA 17019
717-766-8352

Shaw Orchards
21901 Barrens Road South
Stewartstown, PA 17363
717-993-2974
www.shaworchards.com

Silent Springs Farm
Near Routes 216 and 516
Glen Rock, PA 17327
717-235-2128

S. K. Harding and Son
2590 Cape Horn Road
Red Lion, PA 17356
717-755-9528

Sonshine Acres Produce
Joseph Road
York, PA 17404
717-225-4921

*Susquehanna Orchards
Orchard Road
Delta, PA 17314
717-456-7198

Swamp Fox Farms
13517 Country Club Road
Glen Rock, PA 17327
717-235-2685

Tail's End Family Farm
249 Winterstown Road
Red Lion, PA 17356
717-244-7197

Tintagel Farm
Route 216
Brodbecks, PA 17329
717-235-2814

Tri-K Farms
Stamper Road
Brogue, PA 17309
717-927-9624

Triple L Farms
Bonair Road
Glen Rock, PA 17327
717-227-0212

Whitecomb's Produce
and Greenhouses
Roosevelt Avenue
York, PA 17404
717-767-4742

Windy Hill Orchard
1180 Highland Drive
Mechanicsburg, PA 17055
717-766-8509

Wolf's Fruit Farm
998 South Mountain Road
Dillsburg, PA 17019
717-432-3382

Further Reading

Berkley, Robert. *Apples: A Cookbook.* New Jersey: Chartwell Books, 1997.
Browning, Frank. *Apples.* New York: North Point Press, 1998.
Bultitude, John. *Apples: A Guide to the Identification of International Varieties.* London: Macmillan, 1983.
Christensen, Janet M. *Apple Orchard Cookbook.* Stockbridge, Massachusetts: Berkshire Traveller Press, 1992.
Gibbons, Phebe Earle. *Pennsylvania Dutch and Other Essays.* Mechanicsburg, PA: Stackpole Books, 2001.
Hendrick, U. P. *A History of Horticulture in America.* Portland, Oregon: Timber Press, 1988.
Martin, Alice A. *All about Apples.* Boston: Houghton-Mifflin, 1976.
Morgan, Joan, and Alison Richards. *The Book of Apples.* London: Ebury Press, 1993.
Munson, Shirley, and Jo Nelson. *Apple Lovers' Cook Book.* Port Orchard, Washington: Golden West Publishers, 1989.
Orton, Vrest. *The American Cider Book.* New York: Farrar, Straus and Giroux, 1995.
Patent, Greg. *A Is for Apple.* New York: Broadway Books, 1999.
Price, Robert. *Johnny Appleseed, Man and Myth.* Gloucester, Massachusetts: Peter Smith, 1967.
Robertson, Adele C. *The Orchard.* New York: Metropolitan Books, 1995.
Rosentein, Mark. *In Praise of Apples: A Harvest of History, Horticulture and Recipes.* Asheville, North Carolina: Lark Books, 1999.

Sanders, R. *The Apple Book.* New York: Philosophical Library, Inc., 1988.

Toussaint-Samat, Maguelonne. *The History of Food.* Cambridge, Massachusetts: Blackwell, 1994.

Weaver, William Woys. *Sauerkraut Yankees: Pennsylvania Dutch Foods and Foodways.* 2nd Ed. Mechanicsburg, PA: Stackpole Books, 2002.

Woodier, Olwen. *The Apple Cookbook.* Pownal, Vermont: Garden Way, 1989.

Wynne, P. *Apples.* New York: Hawthorn Books, Inc., 1975.

Yepsen, R. *Apples.* New York: W. W. Norton and Company, 1994.

Yoder, Don. *Discovering American Folklife: Essays on Folk Culture and the Pennsylvania Dutch.* Mechanicsburg, PA: Stackpole Books, 2001.